I0755265

HUME'S HISTORY OF ENGLAND. From the latest London trade-edition, reprinted on large type to correspond with the London edition of Macaulay's History. 6 vols, 8vo, cloth. $9.

"These volumes are honorable to the taste, enterprise, and liberality of the publishers, and creditable to the country." — *Boston Atlas.*

"A finer library edition of the great historian of England we have never seen." — *New York Commercial Advertiser.*

ENCYCLOPÆDIA BRITANNICA. Eighth edition, revised, enlarged, and brought up to the present time. Edited by Thomas Stewart Traill, M. D., F. R. S. E., Professor of Medical Jurisprudence in the University of Edinburgh. With upwards of five hundred engravings on steel, and many thousands on wood. To be comprised in 21 vols. 4to. Vols. I. II. and III. now ready. Cloth. $5.50 per volume.

*** This edition has undergone careful revision and extensive alterations, so as to accommodate it to the improved taste and advanced intelligence of the times. The editor has secured the co-operation of the most eminent living authors, who have contributed treatises in the various departments of Science, Literature, the Arts, Manufactures, Commerce, Statistics, and General Knowledge, to supersede those now rendered obsolete by the progress of discovery, improvements in the arts, or the general advancement of society.

MEMOIRS AND CORRESPONDENCE OF FRANCIS HORNER, M.P. Edited by his Brother, Leonard Horner, Esq., F.R.S. 2 vols. 8vo, cloth. $4.50.

MACKINTOSH'S LIFE. — Memoirs of the Life of the Right Honorable Sir James Mackintosh. Edited by his Son, Robert James Mackintosh. From the second London edition. Portrait. 2 vols. 8vo, cloth. $4.50.

"More choice, indeed, than the English edition, and quite worthy of a book so agreeable and popular." — *Daily Advertiser.*

WILKINSON'S ANCIENT EGYPTIANS. — A Popular Account of the Ancient Egyptians. Revised and abridged from his larger work. By Sir J. Gardner Wilkinson. Illustrated with five hundred wood-cuts. 2 vols. post 8vo, cloth. $3.

CARTAPHILUS. — Chronicles selected from the Originals of Cartaphilus, the Wandering Jew, embracing a period of nearly six centuries. Now first revealed to and edited by David Hoffman. Vols. I. and II. 8vo, cloth. $5 per vol. (Vol. III. in press.)

"Mr. Hoffman has succeeded in producing a volume of intense interest." — *English Review.*

HEBER'S (BISHOP) POETICAL WORKS. Uniform with the Aldine Poets. Portrait. Fifth edition. Foolscap 8vo, cloth. $1.25.

RAMSHORN'S LATIN SYNONYMES. — Dictionary of Latin Synonymes. For the use of Schools and Private Students. With a complete Index. By Lewis Ramshorn. Translated from the German by Francis Lieber. New edition. 1 vol. 12mo, half morocco. $1.

WINTHROP'S HISTORY OF NEW ENGLAND. — History of New England, from 1630 to 1649. By John Winthrop, first Governor of the Colony of the Massachusetts Bay. From his original manuscript. With Notes by James Savage. New edition. 2 vols. 8vo, cloth. $4.50.

NORTON'S GENUINENESS OF THE GOSPELS. — Evidences of the Genuineness of the Gospels. By Andrews Norton. Second edition. 3 vols. 8vo, cloth. $5.

NORTON'S TRACTS ON CHRISTIANITY. — Tracts concerning Christianity. By Andrews Norton. 1 vol. 8vo, cloth. $1.50.

ELIOT'S HISTORY OF LIBERTY.— History of Liberty. Part I.: The Ancient Romans. Part II.: The Early Christians. By Samuel Eliot. 4 vols. 12mo, cloth. $5.

BANCROFT'S HISTORY. — History of the United States. Vols. IV. and V., being vols. I. and II. of the History of the Revolution. By Hon. George Bancroft. 8vo, cloth.

"His work is and must be the standard history of the country, and as such should reach every family, and be studied by every person who would be acquainted with the events of our past existence." — *New Haven Journal.*

"The further this work proceeds, the more do we feel that it must take its place as an essentially satisfactory History of the United States." — *London Athenæum.*

SPARKS'S CORRESPONDENCE OF THE REVOLUTION. Being Letters from Eminent Men to George Washington, from the Time of his taking Command of the American Army to the End of his Life. Edited by Jared Sparks. 4 vols. 8vo, cloth, $9; royal 8vo, $12.

SOCIAL THEORIES. — Considerations on some Recent Social Theories. 16mo, cloth. 75 cts.

PARKER'S THEISM. — Sermons of Theism, Atheism, and the Popular Theology. By Theodore Parker. 1 vol. 12mo, cloth. $1.25.

THE BREUGHEL BROTHERS. Translated from the German of the Baron Von Sternberg. By Dr. G. Henry Lodge. Illustrated by Billings. Small 4to, cloth. $2.

MISCELLANEOUS WORKS IN PRESS.

BACON'S WORKS. — The Works of Francis, Lord Bacon. From the complete English edition, by Basil Montague. 12 vols. 8vo.

PLUTARCH'S LIVES. Partly from Dryden's Translation, and partly from other hands. The whole carefully revised and corrected. With some Original Translations by the editor, A. H. Clough, Esq., late Fellow of Oriel College, Oxford. 5 vols. 8vo.

HUME'S PHILOSOPHICAL WORKS. — The Philosophical Writings of David Hume. 4 vols. 8vo.

NORTON'S TRANSLATION OF THE GOSPELS. — A Translation of the Four Gospels. With Notes. By Andrews Norton. 2 vols. 8vo.

PIERCE'S MECHANICS. — A Treatise on Analytic Mechanics. By Benjamin Pierce, LL.D., Perkins Professor of Astronomy and Mathematics in Harvard University. 1 vol. 4to.

DON QUIXOTE. Translated from the Spanish by Motteux. With a Life of the Author, and copious Notes. By J. G. Lockhart. 4 vols. 12mo.

ADAMS'S WORKS. — Life and Works of John Adams, second President of the United States. Edited by his Grandson, Charles Francis Adams. Vols. I. and X.

AMES'S LIFE AND WORKS. — The Life and Works of Fisher Ames. Edited by his Son, Seth Ames, Esq. 2 vols. 8vo.

LYELL'S MANUAL OF GEOLOGY. New edition. — Manual of Elementary Geology; or, the Ancient Changes of the Earth and its Inhabitants, as illustrated by Geological Monuments. By Sir Charles Lyell. Fifth and entirely revised edition. Illustrated with maps, plates, and wood-cuts. 8vo, cloth. (Nearly ready.)

THE POETICAL WORKS OF WILLIAM FALCONER.

WITH A LIFE,

BY REV. JOHN MITFORD.

BOSTON:
LITTLE, BROWN AND COMPANY.
NEW YORK:
EVANS AND DICKERSON.
PHILADELPHIA:
LIPPINCOTT, GRAMBO AND COMPANY.
M.DCCC.LIV.

CAMBRIDGE:
PRINTED BY ALLEN AND FARNHAM.

STEREOTYPED BY STONE AND SMART.

TO

SIR NICHOLAS HARRIS NICOLAS, K. C. M. G.

THIS EDITION OF

FALCONER'S POEMS

IS

WITH EVERY FRIENDLY FEELING

INSCRIBED.

SONNET.

OH! thou storm-beaten Harp! whom erst the wave,
As in despite flung from the greedy sea,
When the ship-foundering tempest hung on thee,
Rock-built Colonna! — Mockery to save;
While the Mosambique, hungry as the grave,
Howl'd o'er the midnight surges for his prey.
So are they gone, each favouring deity,
And not a conch is sounding from the cave,
Of the god-peopled ocean! — Hark, the strain,
That won the gentle dolphin to display
Congenial love, and far from death his prey
Bear o'er the charmèd billow. — Ah! in vain,
Tuneful Arion! is thy dying lay
Along the silver waters heard again.

J. MITFORD.

Benhall, June 1, 1836.

CONTENTS.

THE SHIPWRECK.

THE LIFE OF WILLIAM FALCONER.

BY THE REV. JOHN MITFORD.

WHEN Anderson published the life of Falconer, the earliest which I have seen, in his collection of the British Poets, he possessed,* as he confesses, no memorials of the birthplace or parentage of the poet: and when Stanier Clarke was preparing his accurate and beautiful edition, he was equally at a loss for authentic materials, till he fortunately met with Governor Hunter, a shipmate of the poet's, at the house of Mr. M'Arthur. From the communications of this gentleman, and from subsequent conversations with his brother, Lieutenant Hunter, of Greenwich Hospital, many particulars were collected: Clarke's Life of Falconer has justly been the foundation on which Mr. Chalmers's, and all subsequent biographies have been founded, and, with some trifling additions, it must be the one to which the present will look, as to its most correct authority.

* Anderson's edition of the British Poets was published in 1795. Mr. Stanier Clarke's edition of the Shipwreck, in 1806.

William Falconer, who has given lasting dignity to a name previously obscure, was born about 1736* or 1737, and was the son of a poor man at Edinburgh, who exercised the equally unprofitable trades of barber and wig-maker in the Netherbow, and subsequently of grocer: he got no more by weighing plums than by shaving polls: he was also a fellow of infinite wit, and consequently remained "an honest poor man" as long as he lived.

The vocal powers of the family, which are generally shared largely by the female members, were in this instance concentrated in the person of our poet: for his brothers and sisters were *all* deaf or dumb: and Captain Hunter verified the statement which Falconer had made to him of this unusual infliction, when he met two of the family in the poor-house at Edinburgh, where they continued until death. Falconer received some education which may truly be called *Elementary*, at the school of a Mr. Webster, for the establishment was broken up in 1746, when he was only *beginning his grammar*, and there is no reason to suppose that he went to any other. The following account of him is from the pen of Mr. Forrest: "I well remember being greatly surprised when he gave me a copy of the above ode (On the Prince of Wales) as his own, for he had been always reckoned rather a dunce at

* Mr. J. Forrest, the correspondent of Dr. Anderson, printed in Campbell's History of Scottish Poetry, 4to. 1798, p. 237.

school; and, young as I then was, I knew that a sailor's life was not favourable for the cultivation of letters. I never to my recollection saw him since that time, indeed I fancy he never was here. He was a lumpish, heavy looking lad, very careless and dirty in his dress, and was known by the appellation of Bubly-hash-Falconer; if you are not a Scotchman, this name will not convey to you such a distinct idea of his looks as it does to one of us." * He was then placed, reluctantly on his part, on board a merchant vessel at Leith, and there he served his apprenticeship.†

> Forlorn of heart and by severe decree,
> Condemn'd RELUCTANT to the faithless sea.

One of his biographers ‡ asserts that the affairs of his father, which were never prosperous, fell into great derangement on the death of his wife, a woman whose prudent management had long averted the impending crisis. Subsequently he was servant to Archibald Campbell, the author of Lexiphanes and other works, who was purser of a ship. Dr. Currie, in his edition of Burns, § says "that his master

* See Al. Campbell's Introd. of Poetry to Scotland, p. 237.

† See Lives of the Scottish Poets, 1822, 3 vols. Boys, vol. iii. p. 64. Although a Life of Falconer by Irving is alluded to by his biographers, I can find none in my copy of Irving's Lives of the Scottish Poets, 2 vols. 8vo. Ed. 1804.

‡ For an account of Campbell, see Dyce's Akenside, p. lxxix. Hawkins's Life of Johnson, p. 347.

§ See Currie's ed. of Burns, vol. ii. p. 283, 2nd ed.

delighted to instruct the mind of the young seaman, and boasted of his tuition, when Falconer subsequently had acquired reputation." It is supposed that through Campbell's interest, Falconer was made second mate of a vessel employed in the Levant trade, (the Britannia,) which was shipwrecked in her passage from Alexandria to Venice, near Cape Colonna, on the coast of Greece.

The exact date when this calamity happened, is not known; only three of the crew survived — and the distressing event made such an impression on Falconer's mind, as to become the subject of a poem; which certainly is not, as Stanier Clarke asserts, one of the finest in our language, and is far from being so; but which in all probability will continue to be a favourite with a certain class of readers, and therefore preserve its station among the brotherhood of English Poets.

In 1751, Falconer, as an humble sailor, for he had not risen above that station, revisited his native city, and commenced his poetical career with an elegy on the death of Frederick, Prince of Wales; Gray also began his, with an Hymeneal on the marriage of the same illustrious person. He followed up his first step on the poetic ladder, with others; and sent to the Gentleman's Magazine, (which has been the kind protector of all youthful bards, and in whose venerable courts they have imped their plumes, and tried their earliest flights), a few poems, that have been recognized as his — as * The Chaplain's Petition to the Lieutenants in the Ward Room — The Description of a Ninety-gun Ship — and some lines containing a very unusual and unnecessary complaint — *On the Uncommon Scarcity of Poets.* — These are given to Falconer on the authority of Dr. Clarke, who also is of opinion, that he was the author of the popular song — Cease, rude Boreas,† — and another copy of verses, descriptive of the sentiments and abode of a midshipman, has been ascribed to him by the same biographer.

Falconer is supposed to have continued in the merchant service till he published his poem of the Shipwreck in 1762,‡ which was dedicated to the

* See Gent. Mag. 1758, p. 371. This poem Lieutenant Hunter ascribed to Falconer; the other two are given on the belief of S. Clarke: it is not of much consequence from whom such lines as the following proceeded: —

The rough rude wind which stern Æŏlus sends.

† This is a mere conjecture of S. Clarke's, who thinks the song to be either Falconer's, or Captain Thomson's, the well known editor of several works, as well as author of some popular naval songs. See also 'The Songs of England and Scotland, 2 vols. 1835,' vol. i. p. 231, and Naval Chronicle, vol. ii. p. 233, where the song is decidedly attributed to Falconer, and said "to have been long given with singular injustice to G. Al. Steevens."

‡ The first edition was printed by Miller in May, 1762. Shipwreck, in Three Cantos, by a Sailor, 4to. The subsequent editions, says Mr. Alex. Campbell, are by many deemed inferior to the first, as what it has gained in embellishment it has lost in

Duke of York, who had hoisted his flag as rear admiral of the Blue, on board the Princess Amelia, attached to the fleet under Sir Edward Hawke. Clarke says, "the author was deservedly called a second Homer." The Duke of York kindly patronized this unlooked for production of a sailor, and advised Falconer to leave the merchant service for the Royal Navy. He was accordingly rated as a midshipman on board Sir Edward Hawke's ship, the Royal George; perhaps the very same ship, the funeral knell of which was so musically tolled by the Bard of Olney. In his last visit to Scotland, after the publication of the Shipwreck, it has been said that Falconer * resided at the Manse of Glads-

true poetical beauty, and energy of expression. "There is frequently a copious simplicity," says Dr. Anderson, "in his first designs, that no after thought or labour can amend; an irregular beauty, that every alteration must efface."

* See Lives of Scottish Poets, v. iii. p. 74. The same writer also observes that Falconer was on board the Ramillies, Captain Taylor, with Admiral Bressau's squadron, Dec. 1760, was shipwrecked, coming up the channel, and out of a crew of 734 men, only Falconer and twenty-three others escaped. These circumstances are not in Dr. Clarke's narrative. It was on this wreck of the Ramillies, and not of the Britannia, that this biographer supposes the poem to be founded: vide Lives, v. iii. p. 70. I shall give his argument in his own words, observing that he is the only biographer of Falconer who alludes to the poet being on board the Ramillies; nor does Dr. Clarke assign the poem in Gent. Mag. dated Ramillies, B. of Biscay, 25th Nov. 1706, to Falconer, which the present writer does. He *supposes* that the shipwreck of the *Ramillies* suggested the poem, but that the loss of the *Britannia* was chosen for the sake of the scenery. "It seems

muir, which was then possessed by his illustrious kinsman, Dr. Robertson, whose father was cousin-german to Falconer. Mr. Chalmers, however, remarks on this statement, that though Robertson may have been related to Falconer, he certainly had left Gladsmuir at that time.

The Shipwreck, on its appearance, was reviewed in the Monthly Review, vol. xxvii. p. 197, in a style of criticism which in later times has given way to one less indulgent and encouraging. The praise here bestowed on Falconer, of equalling Virgil in

rather probable that he proceeded by an inverted order, and that his verses on the loss of the Ramillies first gave the idea of the more extended poem, on the loss of the Britannia. The tribute which he paid to the memory of the Prince of Wales, shows what were his poetical powers after his first misfortune; and if we examine the Shipwreck by this test, it will be found that there is scarcely a couplet in it which can be referred *to so humble a level.* It displays everywhere proofs of having been begun and ended during a far more advanced period of improvement, when he had acquired an *astonishing mastery* over the mechanism of versification, and was rich in ideas, the fruit of long experience and reflection. It is deserving too of attention, that in many places the story has evidently been indebted for circumstances that heighten its interest, to what the *author could only* have witnessed on board the Ramillies: and though it is possible that these may have been additions to a poem previously written, yet there is an air of original connectedness in the narrative, which by no means favours the supposition. The throwing the guns overboard is one very striking instance of that *Man-of-war* experience which pervades the poem: nor could any thing but the latitude of poetical license justify the introduction of such a circumstance into the description of a merchant vessel in distress." This writer's reasons must be taken for what they are worth.

his descriptions, and surpassing him in the character of the modern Palinurus, is such, as in the present day would hardly have been bestowed on our most honoured poets; and Dr. Clarke has added, while giving some passages which an Irishman had translated into Latin verse, "that they will prove, *even to the pedant*, that the diction between Virgil and Falconer is not so great as may be imagined." Truly the comparison of Falconer's somewhat prosaic lines, translated into Hibernian Latin, to Virgil's exquisite and inimitable language, is most wonderfully unfortunate! But we proceed to give the review:—

"It has frequently been observed, that true genius will surmount every obstacle which opposes its exertion: how unfavourable soever the situation of a Seaman may be thought to the Poet, certain it is the two characters are not incompatible; for none but an able Seaman could give so didactic an account, and so accurate a description of the voyage and catastrophe here related; and none but a particular favourite of the muses could have embellished both with equal harmony of numbers, and strength of imagery.

"The main subject of the poem is the loss of the Ship Britannia, a merchantman, bound from Alexandria to Venice, which touched at the Island of Candia; whence proceeding on her voyage, she met with a violent storm that drove her on the coasts of

Greece, where she suffered shipwreck near Cape Colonne; three only of the crew being left alive.

"The ship putting to sea from the Port of Candia, the Poet takes an opportunity of making several beautiful marine descriptions; such as the prospect of the shore; a shoal of dolphins; a water-spout; the method of taking an azimuth; and working the ship. In the Second Canto, the ship having cleared the land, the storm begins; and with it the consultation of the pilots, and operations of the seamen; all which the Poet has described with an amazing minuteness, and has found means to reduce the several technical terms of the marine into smooth and harmonious numbers. Homer has been admired by some for reducing a catalogue of ships into tolerably flowing verse; but who, except a poetical Sailor, the nursling of Apollo, educated by Neptune, would ever have thought of versifying his own sea-language? what other poet would ever have dreamt of *reef-tackles*, *haliards*, *clue-garnets*, *buntlines*, *lashings*, *laniards*, and fifty other terms equally obnoxious to the soft sing-song of modern poetasters.

"Many of his descriptions are not inferior to any thing in the Æneid; many passages in the third and fifth books of which our Author has had in view; they have not suffered by his imitation; and his pilot appears to much greater advantage than the Palinurus of Virgil.

"Nor is the Poet's talent confined to the description of inanimate scenes: he relates, and bewails, the untimely fate of his companions in the most animated and pathetic strains. The close of the master's address to the seamen, in the time of their greatest danger, is noble and philosophical. It is impossible to read the circumstantial account of the unfortunate end of the ship's crew, without being deeply affected by the tale, and charmed with the manner of the relation."

At the peace of 1763, the Royal George was paid off, but Falconer had previously published an ode entitled, On the Duke of York's Second Departure from England as Rear Admiral. He composed it, as Governor Hunter observed, during an occasional absence from his messmates, when he retired into a small space between the cable trees and the ship's side. Dr. Clarke considers the conclusion to be not unworthy of Dryden; but I confess I can see no marks of that divine hand. It was severely reviewed in the Critical Review, which very review Dr. Clarke says was written by Falconer. This, on all rational grounds was very improbable; and Mr. Chalmers has on competent authority contradicted it.

Falconer now exchanged the military for the civil department of the navy; and in 1763, he was appointed purser of the Glory frigate of 32 guns. Soon after, he married a young lady of the unpoetical name of Hicks, the daughter of a surgeon of Sheerness Yard. Mr. T. Campbell* says, "she was an accomplished and *beautiful* woman:" the last quality is entirely derived from the biographer's gallantry; for Dr. Clarke says, that it was rather the lustre of Miss Hicks's mind, than the beauty of her person, that attracted the enamoured poet. She possessed talents which she inherited; and the marriage turned out to the happiness of the parties. When Dr. Clarke was collecting materials for his Life, he could not discover where Falconer's widow resided; but he considered that she probably possessed a miniature,† and letters of her husband, which would have thrown light on his history. Mr. Chalmers, who was writing in 1810, says, that she died at Bath a few years since, and was liberally supplied with money by Mr. Cadell in consideration of the successful sale of her husband's marine dictionary. The doubts and distractions of the poet's courtship were expressed in a ballad called the Fond Lover; by which it would appear that the fort of Miss Hicks's affection and virtue did not surrender till after a doubtful and protracted siege. He poured forth his sorrows, as all distressed servants

* See T. Campbell's Specimens of the British Poets, vol. vi. p. 97. Miss Hicks's poetical name was "Miranda." Ritson has praised Falconer's Address to Miranda, "The smiling plains profusely gay," &c.

† No picture or likeness of Falconer is known to exist.

of Apollo have done since the days of Homer, to the winds and waves:

> ——Sadly social with my lay
> The winds in concert weep.

and again,

> Since all her thoughts by sense refined,
> Unartful truth express;
> Say, wherefore sense and truth are join'd
> To give my soul distress?

When the Glory was laid up in ordinary at Chatham, Commissioner Hanway, brother to the celebrated Jonas Hanway, took an interest in the poetical talents and pursuits of the purser; and the captain's cabin was ordered to be fitted up with all comforts and conveniences, that Falconer might pursue his studies without expense. Here he finished his Marine Dictionary—a work of years—the design was suggested to him by Mr. Scott, and approved by Sir Edward Hawke. The celebrated Du Hamel, who had distinguished himself for some writings on naval architecture, also gave it his approbation. Those published on similar subjects abroad, he described as being very imperfect:—'Ce livre manquoit absolument.'—From the Glory Falconer was appointed to the Swiftsure. In 1764, he published a new edition of his poem, with corrections and additions. The next year he printed a political satire on Lord Chatham, Wilks, Churchill,

&c. which Dr. Clarke says was a proper antidote to the *Rosciad!* it might as well have been an antidote to Paradise Lost.

The Marine Dictionary was published in 1769, and Falconer left his commodious cabin, for one of those abodes of genius — the poet's rightful inheritance — a garret in the metropolis. Here he struggled on in some way or other, the particulars of which are not known; at length he received a proposal from Mr. Murray, the bookseller, to join with him in taking Mr. Sandby's business opposite St. Dunstan's Church. The offer, as it appears by Murray's letter, seemed to hold out prospects of great advantage: why Falconer did not accept it, does not appear: if he had, the splendid and successful establishment in Albemarle Street, the offspring of the other, might now have been graced with a poet's name. Speaking of the publishing booksellers, Mr. Murray writes — "Many blockheads in the trade are making fortunes, and did we not succeed as well as they, I think it must be imputed only to ourselves."

A third edition of the Shipwreck being called for in 1769, considerable improvements and additions were prepared by the author: but being appointed purser to the Aurora Frigate, which was going out to India, with Mr. Vansittart,* and others, as com-

* It is said, Mr. Falconer was promised the private secretaryship to the commissioners. See Lives of Sc. Poets, iii. p. 75.

missioners for the company's affairs, in the hurry of his preparations and departure, it is supposed that he left the care of the new edition to his friend Mallet. It is said, that there are some mistakes in the nautical terms; and Dr. Clarke says, "the inferiority of many passages is strikingly evident,"— but if David Mallet the poet is the person alluded to, he was one to whom the fame of the poem might have been safely entrusted; for he was skilled in all the art of versification, and is not likely to have let negligences or errors escape his notice.

We are now drawing to the melancholy and unexpected close of our author's life. The Aurora left England on the 30th Sept. 1769, and after touching at the Cape, which she left on the 27th December, was lost in some part of her remaining passage. It has been supposed that this unfortunate vessel perished by fire: but the more general opinion seems to be, that she foundered in the Mosambique Channel. Captain Lee,* although a stranger to its navigation, would not be dissuaded from attempting it: and it is said, that Mr. Vansittart, who

Mr. Alex. Campbell says, "It should seem from a note subjoined to an address to his mistress, first printed in Dr. Gilbert Stuart's Edinburgh Magazine and Review for November, 1773, that Falconer had been *several times in India*, and it is not improbable, but that his talents had gained him patronage, in consequence of which his appointment in the *Aurora* was such as might have ensured his fortune and independence." — v. Introd. p. 238.

* See Gent. Mag. vol. xli. p. 237.

went out in it, as commissioner, was so averse to this dangerous experiment, that if another ship had been at the Cape, he would have proceeded in her. On the 19th November, 1773, a Black was examined before the board of directors, who affirmed — That he was one of five persons who had been saved from the wreck of the Aurora: that the said frigate had been cast away on a reef of rocks off Macao. That he was two years on an island after he escaped, and was miraculously preserved by a coasting ship happening to touch upon the island. "Falconer," (says Burns, in a letter to Mrs. Dunlop) "the unfortunate author of the Shipwreck, which you so much admire, is no more. After weathering the dreadful catastrophe he so feelingly describes in his poem, and after weathering many hard gales of fortune, he went to the bottom with the Aurora frigate! I forget what part of Scotland had the honour of giving him birth, but he was the son of obscurity and misfortune. He was one of those daring, adventurous spirits, which Scotland beyond any other country is remarkable for producing. Little does the fond mother think, as she hangs delighted over the sweet little leech at her bosom, where the poor fellow may hereafter wander, and what may be his fate. I remember a stanza in an old Scottish ballad, which, notwithstanding its rude simplicity, speaks feelingly to the heart: —

"'Little did my mother think,
That day she cradled me,
What land I was to travel on,
Or what death I should die!'"

In person, Falconer was about five feet two inches in height, of a thin, light make, with hard features, and a weather-beaten complexion. His hair was brown, and he was marked with the smallpox. In his common address, it is said, he was blunt and forbidding: but quick and fluent in conversation. His observation was keen, and his judgments acute and severe. By natural temper he was cheerful, and used to amuse his companions, the seamen, with acrostics which he made on their favourite nymphs. He was a good and skilful seaman. As for education, he assured Governor Hunter, that it was confined to reading, English, and arithmetic. In his voyages, he had picked up a little colloquial knowledge of Italian and Spanish, and such languages as are spoken on the shores of the Mediterranean. That he was esteemed by his mess-mates is shown in a passage of a little work, called the Journal of a Seaman, written in 1755, published by Murray in 1815. "How often," says the author, "have I wished to have the associate of my youth, Bill Falconer, with me to explore these beauties, and to read them in his sweet poetry. But, alas! I parted with him in Old England, never perhaps to meet more in this world. His may be a happier lot, led by a gentler star, he may pass through this busy scene with more ease and tranquillity than has been the fortune of his humble friend, Penrose." *

In considering the merits of the poem of The Shipwreck, it is necessary to dismiss from our minds the exaggerated praises which are to be met with in the pages of some of his editors, as Dr. S. Clarke and Mr. Chalmers, neither of whom, as appears to me, had any pretensions to be considered judges of poetical excellence. If the poem is estimated by a judgment lying between its positive merits, and the disadvantages under which it was composed,—undoubtedly the author will receive no slight proportion of praise. And though, with the exception of some happier parts, it cannot satisfy the taste which has been formed on the finished writings of our leading poets, yet it is a singularly elegant production of a person who had received no education beyond the mere elements of language, and who was subsequently occupied in the severe duties and business of a seafaring life — equally without learning or leisure. The poetical powers of Falconer, in whatever rank they may be placed, were the gift of nature; for any assistance they may have derived from subsequent application, was only a proof that the original powers previously existed.

* See Lives of the Scottish Poets, 1822, vol. iii. p. 77. The life of Falconer is signed R. E. It is doubtful whether this journal of Penrose is real or fictitious. — v. Quarterly Rev.

The Milton of the village remained neither mute, nor inglorious.*

The plan of the poem is simple, but not defective; though it is not difficult to see that it might have been improved by a greater diversity of character, and a more powerful and animated variety of description: in fact, there is not much to praise in the curiosity of the design, or the complication of circumstances through which it was conducted: but though inartificial, it is not carelessly or inefficiently arranged. That the description of the general distress, which has occupied the mind of the reader through the former portion of the poem, should at last merge in the narration of particular and personal history, as in the case of Palæmon, was justly and happily conceived, and thus a dramatic character is drawn over the close. It is agreed that the nautical descriptions are appropriate and correct. The great fault of the poem is one that extends through its entire composition, and consists in the absence of any very striking, and original bursts of genius, — of that fresh and vivid colouring which is given by a bright imagination, — and of those beautiful combinations, happy associations, and masterly touches of the great masters of song. It is true, that Falconer is not an imitator of his predecessors, or a mannerist in any particular school of poetry.

* "Some mute, inglorious Milton here may rest." — *Gray.*

There are no favorite expressions, nor turns of language, nor descriptions copied from preceding poets; his style is not an echo of any other writer. It is most probable that he had studied Pope's Homer, which was the storehouse of all succeeding poets, and the style, language, combinations of words, and tone and modulation of which, descended from poet to poet, till it became at one time a conventional form of poetical speech. There are a few marks in his poem, just sufficient to show that Falconer was not unacquainted with Pope's writings: and he had read sufficiently to make himself familiar with the language of poetry in his day: indeed much of the flatness and tameness of his expressions arises from his use of this long worn, and current coin of Parnassus.

Mr. Campbell has justly observed,—"that his diction too generally abounds with common place expletives, and feeble lines,"—of the first, I should point out such as,—black adversity—unspotted truth—trembling order—melting tear—sacred Maro's art—brazen voice of battle—happy plains—and many others of the like kind. Of the latter, such lines as the following:—

> Determin'd from whatever point they rise,
> To trust his fortune to the seas and skies.

and,

> This vast phenomenon whose lofty head.*

* We remember our late lamented friend, the learned transla-

Add to this, that the construction of Falconer's verse is not often vigorous, or musically varied, and that there is an ungraceful change of the past and present tenses. Such are the defects that might be expected, in the work of a person imperfectly educated, and who, though possessing a taste and feeling for poetry, and a power of embodying his ideas in poetical language, yet had not any of those strong and original powers, which can burst through all obstacles, and compensate for all defects. Such *was* Burns, — and such *is* Ebenezer Elliot, the man of all the self-educated poets, since the days of Burns, of the most original powers, the finest imagination, and the most copious and animated style.

There is little in the descriptions of the scenery of Greece, or of the "Isles that crown the Ægean Main," that could not have been written equally well without the aid of personal observation: nothing graphic and local in the touches; and the various allusions to the historic fame, and the heroic characters of Greece, are too faint and general to afford much delight. With regard to the introduction of sea phrases, I agree with Campbell — "That the effect of some of them is to give a definite, and authentic character to his descriptions; but that most of them to a landsman's ear, resembles slang

tor of Plato and Aristotle, repeating to us an Ode to Venus, the first line of which was,

Before I enter on this great affair, etc.

and produces obscurity." — Such appear to me the defects of this poem; yet notwithstanding these, the Shipwreck will probably remain, as it has always been, a popular poem — not popular among the higher classes of society, nor with those who require, for the gratification of their taste, the delicate and curious finish of the perfect artist; or those who can delight alone in the flashes and outbreaks of the most powerful intellects; in the most original conceptions, and the richest combinations of thought and imagery. — But to others, and those perhaps the most numerous, Falconer's poem will always be a source of rational gratification. The subject itself is interesting — the scenery which belongs to it — the descriptions of natural objects — the changes and various aspects of nature — the sunshine and the storm — the calm and the tempest; while the increasing interest of the story — the impending danger of the ship — the courage and constancy of the crew — the vivid descriptions of the terrific storm — these all combine in keeping the attention alive, and awakening strong sympathy in persons whose feelings are easily aroused; which are neither repressed nor stifled by the customs and courtesies of refined society; nor weakened by a too frequent indulgence in stories of fictitious calamity.

There are some elegant and poetical lines scattered through the narrative, as

> Or win the anchor from his dark abode.

Again on the same subject,

Uptorn, reluctant, from its oozy cave
The pond'rous anchor rises on the wave;

and

Prone on the midnight surge with parting breath;

and

Soft as the happy swain's enchanting lay
That pipes among the shades of Endermay;

and

In every look the Paphian graces shine,
Soft breathing o'er his cheek their bloom divine.

There are also some longer passages of superior merit, one or two of which we extract.

Immortal train! who guide the maze of song,
To whom all science, arts, and arms belong,
Who bid the trumpet of eternal fame
Exalt the warrior's and the poet's name,
Or in lamenting elegies express
The varied pang of exquisite distress;
If e'er with trembling hope * I fondly stray'd
In life's fair morn beneath your hallow'd shade,
To hear the sweetly-mournful lute complain,
And melt the heart with ecstasy of pain,
Or listen to the enchanting voice of love,
While all Elysium warbled through the grove;
Oh! by the hollow blast that moans around,
That sweeps the wild harp with a plaintive sound,
By the long surge that foams through yonder cave,
Whose vaults remurmur to the roaring wave;
With living colours give my verse to glow,
The sad memorial of a tale of woe!

* "There they alike in *trembling hope* repose." — *Gray.*

The fate, in lively sorrow to deplore
Of wanderers shipwreck'd on a leeward shore.
  Alas! neglected by the sacred nine,
Their suppliant feels no genial ray divine:
Ah! will they leave Pieria's happy shore,
To plough the tide where wintry tempests roar?
Or shall a youth approach their hallow'd fane,
Stranger to Phœbus and the tuneful train?
Far from the muses' academic grove,
'T was his the vast and trackless deep to rove;
Alternate change of climates has he known,
And felt the fierce extremes of either zone:
Where polar skies congeal th' eternal snow,
Or equinoctial suns forever glow,
Smote by the freezing, or the scorching blast,
"A ship-boy on the high and giddy mast,"
From regions where Peruvian billows roar,
To the bleak coasts of savage Labrador;
From where Damascus, pride of Asian plains,
Stoops her proud neck beneath tyrannic chains,
To where the isthmus, laved by adverse tides,
Atlantic and Pacific seas divides:
But while he measured o'er the painful race
In fortune's wild illimitable chase,
Adversity, companion of his way,
Still o'er the victim hung with iron sway,
Bade new distresses every instant grow,
Marking each change of place with change of woe.

* * * * * *

Such joyless toils, in early youth endured,
The expanding dawn of mental day obscured,
Each genial passion of the soul opprest,
And quench'd the ardour kindling in his breast:
Then censure not severe the native song,
Though jarring sounds the measured verse prolong,
Though terms uncouth offend the softer ear,
Yet truth, and human anguish deign to hear:

No laurel wreaths these lays attempt to claim,
Nor sculptured brass to tell the poet's name.

* * * * * *

O first-born daughter of primeval time!
By whom transmitted down in every clime
The deeds of ages long elapsed are known,
And blazon'd glories spread from zone to zone;
Whose magic breath dispels the mental night,
And o'er the obscured idea pours the light;
Say on what seas, for thou alone canst tell,
What dire mishap a fated ship befell,
Assail'd by tempests, girt with hostile shores?
Arise! approach! unlock thy treasured stores!
Full on my soul the dreadful scene display,
And give its latent horrors to the day.

I shall add to this the character of "Arion," in which the poet himself is designed.

To Rodmond, next in order of command,
Succeeds the youngest of our naval band:
But what avails it to record a name
That courts no rank among the sons of fame;
Whose vital spring had just began to bloom,
When o'er it sorrow spread her sickening gloom?
While yet a stripling, oft with fond alarms
His bosom danced to Nature's boundless charms;
On him fair science dawn'd in happier hour,
Awakening into bloom young Fancy's flower:
But soon Adversity, with freezing blast,
The blossom wither'd, and the dawn o'ercast.
Forlorn of heart, and by severe decree
Condemn'd reluctant to the faithless sea,
With long farewell he left the laurel grove,
Where science, and the tuneful sisters rove.
Hither he wander'd, anxious to explore
Antiquities of nations now no more;

To penetrate each distant realm unknown,
And range excursive o'er the untravell'd zone:
In vain — for rude adversity's command
Still on the margin of each famous land,
With unrelenting ire his steps opposed,
And every gate of hope against him closed.
Permit my verse, ye blest Pierian train!
To call Arion this ill-fated swain:
For like that bard unhappy, on his head
Malignant stars their hostile influence shed:
Both, in lamenting numbers, o'er the deep
With conscious anguish taught the harp to weep;
And both the raging surge in safety bore
Amid destruction, panting to the shore:
This last, our tragic story from the wave
Of dark oblivion, haply, yet may save:
With genuine sympathy may yet complain,
While sad remembrance bleeds at every vein.

Of Falconer's minor poems, it is not necessary to say much; they can do no honour to the author of the Shipwreck. The poem Sacred to the Memory of the Prince of Wales is written in the following style; which may be called the *Old Elegeiac.*

Oh! bear me to some awful silent glade
Where cedars form an unremitting shade;
Where never track of human feet was known,
Where never cheerful light of Phœbus shone;
Where chirping linnets warble tales of love,
And hoarser winds howl murmuring through the grove.
Where some unhappy wretch aye mourns his doom,
Deep melancholy wandering through the gloom;
Where solitude and meditation roam,
And where no dawning glimpse of hope can come;
Place me in such an unfrequented shade,
To speak to none — but with the mighty dead:

To assist the pouring rains with brimful eyes,
And aid hoarse howling Boreas with my sighs.
* * * * * *
Ye powers, and must a prince so noble die?
Whose equal breathes not under the ambient sky.

The poem called the Demagogue is filled with abuse of Lord Chatham in most virulent and unmeasured terms; the language is in many parts inflated, in others, mean and prosaic; of the former the following lines will be an example: —

Methinks I hear the bellowing Demagogue
Dumb-sounding declamations disembogue;
Expressions of immeasurable length,
Whose pompous jargon fills the place of strength.
Where fulminating rumbling eloquence
With loud theatric rage, bombards the sense,
And words deep ranked in horrible array,
Exasperated metaphors convey.

And these again sink into such couplets as the following: —

But all the events collected to relate,
Let us his actions recapitulate.

The ballad of the "Fond Lover" is the most pleasing of his minor productions.

THE DIRGE OF POOR* ARION.

WHAT pale and bleeding youth (while the fell Blast
Howls o'er the wreck, and fainter sinks the cry
Of struggling wretches ere o'erwhelmed they die)
Yet floats upborne upon the driving mast?
O poor Arion! has thy sweetest strain,
That charm'd old Ocean's wildest solitude,
At this dread hour his waves' dark might subdued?
Let Sea-Maids thy reclining head sustain;
And wipe the blood, and briny drops, that soil
Thy locks, and give once more thy wreathed shell
To ring with melody: — Oh fruitless Toil!
Hark! o'er thy head again the tempests swell;
Hark! hark again the storm's black demons yell
More loud; the bellowing deep reclaims his spoil!
Peace! and may weeping Sea-Maids sing the knell.

W. L. BOWLES.

FAREWELL, poor FALCONER! when the dark Sea
Bursts like despair, I shall remember thee;
Nor ever from the sounding beach depart
Without thy music stealing on my heart,
And thinking still I hear dread Ocean say,
Thou hast declared my might, be thou my prey!

W. L. BOWLES.

* Written on the platform at Portsmouth, April 16, 1803.

THE SHIPWRECK,

IN THREE CANTOS.

THE TIME EMPLOYED IN THIS POEM IS ABOUT SIX DAYS.

Quæque ipse miserrima vidi,
Et quorum pars magna fui. — VIRG. ÆN lib. ii.

ADVERTISEMENT TO THE SECOND EDITION,

PUBLISHED BY A. MILLAR, IN OCTAVO, 1764.

WITH A CHART OF THE SHIP'S PATH FROM CANDIA TO CAPE COLONNA.

IT is perhaps necessary to acquaint the public, that the author of this poem designed not at first to enlarge the work with so many notes, and, to avoid this, proposed to refer his readers to any one of the modern dictionaries, which should be thought most proper for explaining the technical terms occasionally mentioned in the poem; but, after strict examination of them all, including a silly inadequate performance that has lately appeared by a sea-officer,* he could by no means recommend their explanations, without forfeiting his claim to the character assumed in the title-page, of which he is much more tenacious than of his reputation as a poet.

Although it is so frequent a practice to take the advantage of public approbation, and raise the price of performances that have been much encouraged, the author chooses to steer in a quite different

* Can a sea-officer be so ignorant as to mistake the names of the most common things in a ship?

channel: it being a considerable time since the first edition sold off, (notwithstanding the high price, and the singularity of the subject,) he might very justly continue the price; but as it deterred a number of the inferior officers of the sea from purchasing it, at their repeated requests it has been printed now in a smaller edition: at the same time, the author is sorry to observe, that the gentlemen of the sea, for whose entertainment it was chiefly calculated, have hardly made one tenth of the purchasers.

ADVERTISEMENT TO THE THIRD EDITION,

DATED FROM SOMERSET HOUSE, OCTOBER 1, 1769, THE YEAR IN WHICH FALCONER SAILED FOR INDIA.

The favourable reception which this performance has hitherto met with from the public, has encouraged the author to give it a strict and thorough revision; in the course of which, he flatters himself, it will be found to have received very considerable improvements.

INTRODUCTION TO THE POEM.

WHILE jarring interests wake the world to arms,
And fright the peaceful vale with dire alarms,
While Albion bids the avenging thunder roll
Along her vassal deep from pole to pole;
Sick of the scene, where war with ruthless hand
Spreads desolation o'er the bleeding land;
Sick of the tumult, where the trumpet's breath
Bids ruin smile, and drowns the groan of death;
'Tis mine, retired beneath this cavern hoar
That stands all lonely on the sea-beat shore,
Far other themes of deep distress to sing
Than ever trembled from the vocal string;
A scene from dumb oblivion to restore,
To fame unknown, and new to epic lore
Where hostile elements conflicting rise,
And lawless surges swell against the skies,
Till hope expires, and peril and dismay
Wave their black ensigns on the watery way.
Immortal train! who guide the maze of song,

To whom all science, arts, and arms belong,
Who bid the trumpet of eternal fame
Exalt the warrior's and the poet's name,
Or in lamenting elegies express
The varied pang of exquisite distress;
If e'er with trembling hope I fondly stray'd
In life's fair morn beneath your hallow'd shade,
To hear the sweetly-mournful lute complain,
And melt the heart with ecstasy of pain,
Or listen to the enchanting voice of love,
While all Elysium warbled through the grove;
Oh! by the hollow blast that moans around,
That sweeps the wild harp with a plaintive sound;
By the long surge that foams through yonder cave,
Whose vaults remurmur to the roaring wave;
With living colours give my verse to glow,
The sad memorial of a tale of woe!
The fate, in lively sorrow, to deplore
Of wanderers shipwreck'd on a leeward shore.

Alas! neglected by the sacred Nine,
Their suppliant feels no genial ray divine:
Ah! will they leave Pieria's happy shore,
To plough the tide where wintry tempests roar?
Or shall a youth approach their hallow'd fane,
Stranger to Phœbus, and the tuneful train?
Far from the muses' academic grove,

'Twas his the vast and trackless deep to rove;
Alternate change of climates has he known,
And felt the fierce extremes of either zone:
Where polar skies congeal the eternal snow,
Or equinoctial suns for ever glow,
Smote by the freezing, or the scorching blast,
"A ship-boy on the high and giddy mast,"
From regions where Peruvian billows roar,
To the bleak coasts of savage Labrador;
From where Damascus, pride of Asian plains,
Stoops her proud neck beneath tyrannic chains,
To where the Isthmus, laved by adverse tides,
Atlantic and Pacific seas divides:
But while he measured o'er the painful race
In fortune's wild illimitable chase,
Adversity, companion of his way,
Still o'er the victim hung with iron sway,
Bade new distresses every instant grow,
Marking each change of place with change of woe:
In regions where the Almighty's chastening hand
With livid pestilence afflicts the land,
Or where pale famine blasts the hopeful year,
Parent of want and misery severe;
Or where, all-dreadful in the embattled line,
The hostile ships in flaming combat join,
Where the torn vessel wind and waves assail,

Till o'er her crew distress and death prevail.—
Such joyless toils, in early youth endured,
The expanding dawn of mental day obscured,
Each genial passion of the soul opprest,
And quench'd the ardour kindling in his breast:
Then censure not severe the native song,
Though jarring sounds the measured verse prolong,
Though terms uncouth offend the softer ear,
Yet truth, and human anguish deign to hear:
No laurel wreaths these lays attempt to claim,
Nor sculptured brass to tell the poet's name.

And lo! the power that wakes the eventful song
Hastes hither from Lethean banks along;
She sweeps the gloom, and, rushing on the sight,
Spreads o'er the kindling scene propitious light:
In her right hand an ample roll appears,
Fraught with long annals of preceding years,
With every wise and noble art of man
Since first the circling hours their course began;
Her left a silver wand on high display'd,
Whose magic touch dispels oblivion's shade:
Pensive her look; on radiant wings that glow
Like Juno's birds, or Iris' flaming bow,
She sails; and swifter than the course of light
Directs her rapid intellectual flight:
The fugitive ideas she restores,

And calls the wandering thought from Lethe's shores;
To things long past a second date she gives,
And hoary time from her fresh youth receives;
Congenial sister of immortal fame,
She shares her power, and memory is her name.
O first-born daughter of primeval time!
By whom transmitted down in every clime
The deeds of ages long elapsed are known,
And blazon'd glories spread from zone to zone;
Whose magic breath dispels the mental night,
And o'er the obscured idea pours the light;
Say on what seas, for thou alone canst tell,
What dire mishap a fated ship befell,
Assail'd by tempests, girt with hostile shores?
Arise! approach! unlock thy treasured stores!
Full on my soul the dreadful scene display,
And give its latent horrors to the day.

FIRST CANTO:

THE SCENE OF WHICH LIES NEAR THE CITY OF CANDIA.

TIME, ABOUT FOUR DAYS AND A HALF.

ARGUMENT.

I. Retrospect of the voyage. Arrival at Candia. State of that island. Season of the year described. — II. Character of the master, and his officers, Albert, Rodmond, and Arion. Palemon, son to the owner of the ship. Attachment of Palemon to Anna, the daughter of Albert. — III. Noon. Palemon's history. — IV. Sunset. Midnight. Arion's dream. Unmoor by moonlight. Morning. Sun's azimuth taken. Beautiful appearance of the ship, as seen by the natives from the shore.

THE SHIPWRECK.

CANTO I.

I. A SHIP from Egypt, o'er the deep impell'd
By guiding winds, her course for Venice held.
Of famed Britannia were the gallant crew,
And from that isle her name the vessel drew;
The wayward steps of fortune they pursued,
And sought in certain ills imagined good:
Though caution'd oft her slippery path to shun,
Hope still with promised joys allured them on;
And, while they listen'd to her winning lore,
The softer scenes of peace could please no more:
Long absent they from friends and native home
The cheerless ocean were inured to roam;
Yet heaven, in pity to severe distress,
Had crown'd each painful voyage with success;
Still to compensate toils and hazards past
Restored them to maternal plains at last.

Thrice had the sun to rule the varying year
Across the equator roll'd his flaming sphere,
Since last the vessel spread her ample sail
From Albion's coast, obsequious to the gale;
She o'er the spacious flood, from shore to shore
Unwearying wafted her commercial store;
The richest ports of Afric she had view'd,
Thence to fair Italy her course pursued;
Had left behind Trinacria's burning isle,
And visited the margin of the Nile:
And now, that winter deepens round the pole,
The circling voyage hastens to its goal:
They, blind to fate's inevitable law,
No dark event to blast their hope foresaw,
But from gay Venice soon expect to steer
For Britain's coast, and dread no perils near;
Inflamed by hope, their throbbing hearts elate
Ideal pleasures vainly antedate,
Before whose vivid intellectual ray
Distress recedes, and danger melts away:
Already British coasts appear to rise,
The chalky cliffs salute their longing eyes;
Each to his breast, where floods of rapture roll,
Embracing strains the mistress of his soul;
Nor less o'erjoy'd, with sympathetic truth,
Each faithful maid expects the approaching youth:

In distant souls congenial passions glow,
And mutual feelings mutual bliss bestow —
Such shadowy happiness their thoughts employ,
Illusion all, and visionary joy!
  Thus time elapsed, while o'er the pathless tide
Their ship through Grecian seas the pilots guide.
Occasion call'd to touch at Candia's shore,
Which, blest with favouring winds, they soon explore;
The haven enter, borne before the gale,
Dispatch their commerce, and prepare to sail.
  Eternal powers! what ruins from afar.
Mark the fell track of desolating war:
Here arts and commerce with auspicious reign
Once breathed sweet influence on the happy plain;
While o'er the lawn, with dance and festive song,
Young pleasure led the jocund hours along;
In gay luxuriance Ceres too was seen
To crown the valleys with eternal green:
For wealth, for valour, courted and revered,
What Albion is, fair Candia then appear'd. —
Ah! who the flight of ages can revoke?
The free-born spirit of her sons is broke,
They bow to Ottoman's imperious yoke;
No longer fame their drooping heart inspires,
For stern oppression quench'd its genial fires:

Tho' still her fields, with golden harvests crown'd,
Supply the barren shores of Greece around,
Sharp penury afflicts these wretched isles,
There hope ne'er dawns, and pleasure never smiles;
The vassal wretch contented drags his chain,
And hears his famish'd babes lament in vain:
These eyes have seen the dull reluctant soil
A seventh year mock the weary labourer's toil.—
No blooming Venus, on the desert shore,
Now views with triumph captive gods adore;
No lovely Helens now with fatal charms
Excite the avenging chiefs of Greece to arms;
No fair Penelopes enchant the eye,
For whom contending kings were proud to die;
Here sullen beauty sheds a twilight ray,
While sorrow bids her vernal bloom decay:
Those charms, so long renown'd in classic strains,
Had dimly shone on Albion's happier plains!
  Now, in the southern hemisphere, the sun
Through the bright Virgin, and the Scales, had run,
And on the ecliptic wheel'd his winding way
Till the fierce Scorpion felt his flaming ray.
Four days becalm'd the vessel here remains,
And yet no hopes of aiding wind obtains;
For sickening vapours lull the air to sleep,
And not a breeze awakes the silent deep:

This, when the autumnal equinox is o'er,
And Phœbus in the north declines no more,
The watchful mariner, whom heaven informs,
Oft deems the prelude of approaching storms.—
No dread of storms the master's soul restrain,
A captive fetter'd to the oar of gain:
His anxious heart, impatient of delay,
Expects the winds to sail from Candia's bay,
Determined, from whatever point they rise,
To trust his fortune to the seas, and skies.
  Thou living ray of intellectual fire,
Whose voluntary gleams my verse inspire,
Ere yet the deepening incidents prevail,
Till roused attention feel our plaintive tale;
Record whom chief among the gallant crew
The unblest pursuit of fortune hither drew:
Can sons of Neptune, generous, brave, and bold,
In pain and hazard toil for sordid gold?
  They can! for gold too oft with magic art
Can rule the passions, and corrupt the heart:
This crowns the prosperous villain with applause,
To whom in vain sad merit pleads her cause;
This strews with roses life's perplexing road,
And leads the way to pleasure's soft abode;
This spreads with slaughter'd heaps the bloody plain,

And pours adventurous thousands o'er the main.
II. The stately ship, with all her daring band,
To skilful Albert own'd the chief command:
Though train'd in boisterous elements, his mind
Was yet by soft humanity refined;
Each joy of wedded love, at home, he knew,
Aboard, confest the father of his crew!
Brave, liberal, just! the calm domestic scene
Had o'er his temper breathed a gay serene:
Him science taught by mystic lore to trace
The planets wheeling in eternal race;
To mark the ship in floating balance held,
By earth attracted, and by seas repell'd;
Or point her devious track through climes unknown
That leads to every shore and every zone:
He saw the moon thro' heaven's blue concave glide,
And into motion charm the expanding tide,
While earth impetuous round her axle rolls,
Exalts her watery zone, and sinks the poles;
Light and attraction, from their genial source,
He saw still wandering with diminish'd force;
While on the margin of declining day
Night's shadowy cone reluctant melts away—
Inured to peril, with unconquer'd soul,
The chief beheld tempestuous oceans roll:
O'er the wild surge when dismal shades preside,

His equal skill the lonely bark could guide;
His genius, ever for the event prepared,
Rose with the storm, and all its dangers shared.
Rodmond the next degree to Albert bore,
A hardy son of England's farthest shore,
Where bleak Northumbria pours her savage train
In sable squadrons o'er the northern main;
That, with her pitchy entrails stored, resort,
A sooty tribe, to fair Augusta's port:
Where'er in ambush lurk the fatal sands,
They claim the danger, proud of skilful bands;
For while with darkling course their vessels sweep
The winding shore, or plough the faithless deep,
O'er bar, and shelve, the watery path they sound
With dexterous arm, sagacious of the ground:
Fearless they combat every hostile wind,
Wheeling in mazy tracks, with course inclined.
Expert to moor where terrors line the road,
Or win the anchor from its dark abode;
But drooping, and relax'd, in climes afar,
Tumultuous and undisciplined in war.
Such Rodmond was; by learning unrefined,
That oft enlightens to corrupt the mind.
Boisterous of manners; train'd in early youth
To scenes that shame the conscious cheek of truth;
To scenes that nature's struggling voice control,

And freeze compassion rising in the soul:
Where the grim hell-hounds, prowling round the shore,
With foul intent the stranded bark explore;
Deaf to the voice of woe, her decks they board,
While tardy justice slumbers o'er her sword.
The indignant muse, severely taught to feel,
Shrinks from a theme she blushes to reveal.
Too oft example, arm'd with poisons fell,
Pollutes the shrine where mercy loves to dwell:
Thus Rodmond, train'd by this unhallow'd crew,
The sacred social passions never knew.
Unskill'd to argue, in dispute yet loud,
Bold without caution, without honours proud;
In art unschool'd, each veteran rule he prized,
And all improvement haughtily despised.
Yet, though full oft to future perils blind,
With skill superior glow'd his daring mind
Through snares of death the reeling bark to guide,
When midnight shades involve the raging tide.
To Rodmond, next in order of command,
Succeeds the youngest of our naval band:
But what avails it to record a name
That courts no rank among the sons of fame;
Whose vital spring had just began to bloom,
When o'er it sorrow spread her sickening gloom?

While yet a stripling, oft with fond alarms
His bosom danced to nature's boundless charms;
On him fair science dawn'd in happier hour,
Awakening into bloom young fancy's flower:
But soon adversity, with freezing blast,
The blossom wither'd, and the dawn o'ercast.
Forlorn of heart, and by severe decree
Condemn'd reluctant to the faithless sea,
With long farewell he left the laurel grove,
Where science, and the tuneful sisters rove.
Hither he wander'd, anxious to explore
Antiquities of nations now no more;
To penetrate each distant realm unknown,
And range excursive o'er the untravell'd zone:
In vain — for rude adversity's command
Still on the margin of each famous land,
With unrelenting ire his steps opposed,
And every gate of hope against him closed.
Permit my verse, ye blest Pierian train!
To call Arion this ill-fated swain;
For like that bard unhappy, on his head
Malignant stars their hostile influence shed:
Both, in lamenting numbers, o'er the deep
With conscious anguish taught the harp to weep;
And both the raging surge in safety bore
Amid destruction, panting to the shore:

This last, our tragic story from the wave
Of dark oblivion, haply, yet may save;
With genuine sympathy may yet complain,
While sad remembrance bleeds at every vein.
These, chief among the ship's conducting train,
Her path explored along the deep domain;
Train'd to command, and range the swelling sail,
Whose varying force conforms to every gale.
Charged with the commerce, hither also came
A gallant youth, Palemon was his name:
A father's stern resentment doom'd to prove,
He came the victim of unhappy love!
His heart for Albert's beauteous daughter bled,
For her a sacred flame his bosom fed:
Nor let the wretched slaves of folly scorn
This genuine passion, nature's eldest born!
'Twas his with lasting anguish to complain,
While blooming Anna mourn'd the cause in vain.
Graceful of form, by nature taught to please,
Of power to melt the female breast with ease;
To her Palemon told his tender tale
Soft as the voice of summer's evening gale:
His soul, where moral truth spontaneous grew,
No guilty wish, no cruel passion knew:
Though tremblingly alive to nature's laws,
Yet ever firm to honour's sacred cause;

O'erjoy'd he saw her lovely eyes relent,
The blushing maiden smiled with sweet consent.
Oft in the mazes of a neighbouring grove
Unheard they breathed alternate vows of love:
By fond society their passion grew,
Like the young blossom fed with vernal dew;
While their chaste souls possess'd the pleasing pains
That truth improves, and virtue ne'er restrains.
In evil hour the officious tongue of fame
Betray'd the secret of their mutual flame.
With grief and anger struggling in his breast,
Palemon's father heard the tale confest;
Long had he listen'd with suspicion's ear,
And learnt, sagacious, this event to fear.
Too well, fair youth! thy liberal heart he knew,
A heart to nature's warm impressions true:
Full oft his wisdom strove with fruitless toil
With avarice to pollute that generous soil;
That soil impregnated with nobler seed
Refused the culture of so rank a weed.
Elate with wealth in active commerce won,
And basking in the smile of fortune's sun;
For many freighted ships from shore to shore,
Their wealthy charge by his appointment bore;
With scorn the parent eyed the lowly shade
That veil'd the beauties of this charming maid.

He, by the lust of riches only moved,
Such mean connexions haughtily reproved;
Indignant he rebuked the enamour'd boy,
The flattering promise of his future joy;
He soothed and menaced, anxious to reclaim
This hopeless passion, or divert its aim:
Oft led the youth where circling joys delight
The ravish'd sense, or beauty charms the sight.
With all her powers enchanting music fail'd,
And pleasure's syren voice no more prevail'd:
Long with unequal art, in vain he strove
To quench the ethereal flame of ardent love.
  The merchant, kindling then with proud disdain,
In look, and voice, assumed a harsher strain.
In absence now his only hope remain'd;
And such the stern decree his will ordain'd:
Deep anguish, while Palemon heard his doom,
Drew o'er his lovely face a saddening gloom;
High beat his heart, fast flow'd the unbidden tear,
His bosom heaved with agony severe;
In vain with bitter sorrow he repined,
No tender pity touch'd that sordid mind—
To thee, brave Albert! was the charge consign'd.
The stately ship forsaking England's shore
To regions far remote Palemon bore.
Incapable of change, the unhappy youth

Still loved fair Anna with eternal truth;
Still Anna's image swims before his sight
In fleeting vision through the restless night;
From clime to clime an exile doom'd to roam,
His heart still panted for its secret home.
  The moon had circled twice her wayward zone,
To him since young Arion first was known;
Who wandering here through many a scene renown'd,
In Alexandria's port the vessel found;
Where, anxious to review his native shore,
He on the roaring wave embark'd once more.
Oft by pale Cynthia's melancholy light
With him Palemon kept the watch of night,
In whose sad bosom many a sigh supprest
Some painful secret of the soul confest:
Perhaps Arion soon the cause divined,
Though shunning still to probe a wounded mind;
He felt the chastity of silent woe,
Though glad the balm of comfort to bestow.
He with Palemon oft recounted o'er
The tales of hapless love in ancient lore,
Recall'd to memory by the adjacent shore:
The scene thus present, and its story known,
The lover sigh'd for sorrows not his own.
Thus, though a recent date their friendship bore,

Soon the ripe metal own'd the quickening ore;
For in one tide their passions seem'd to roll,
By kindred age and sympathy of soul.
 These o'er the inferior naval train preside,
The course determine, or the commerce guide:
O'er all the rest, an undistinguish'd crew,
Her wing of deepest shade oblivion drew.
 III. A sullen languor still the skies opprest,
And held the unwilling ship in strong arrest:
High in his chariot glow'd the lamp of day,
O'er Ida flaming with meridian ray;
Relax'd from toil, the sailors range the shore,
Where famine, war, and storm are felt no more;
The hour to social pleasure they resign,
And black remembrance drown in generous wine.
On deck, beneath the shading canvas spread,
Rodmond a rueful tale of wonders read
Of dragons roaring on the enchanted coast;
The hideous goblin, and the yelling ghost:
But with Arion, from the sultry heat
Of noon, Palemon sought a cool retreat.—
And lo! the shore with mournful prospects crown'd,
The rampart torn with many a fatal wound,
The ruin'd bulwark tottering o'er the strand,
Bewail the stroke of war's tremendous hand:
What scenes of woe this hapless isle o'erspread!

Where late thrice fifty thousand warriors bled.
Full twice twelve summers were yon towers assail'd,
Till barbarous Ottoman at last prevail'd;
While thundering mines the lovely plains o'erturn'd,
While heroes fell, and domes and temples burn'd.
  But now before them happier scenes arise,
Elysian vales salute their ravish'd eyes;
Olive, and cedar, form'd a grateful shade
Where light, with gay romantic error stray'd:
The myrtles here with fond caresses twine,
There, rich with nectar, melts the pregnant vine:
And lo! the stream, renown'd in classic song,
Sad Lethe, glides the silent vale along.
On mossy banks, beneath the citron grove,
The youthful wanderers found a wild alcove;
Soft o'er the fairy region languor stole,
And with sweet melancholy charm'd the soul.
Here first Palemon, while his pensive mind
For consolation on his friend reclined,
In pity's bleeding bosom, pour'd the stream
Of love's soft anguish, and of grief supreme:
"Too true thy words! by sweet remembrance taught,
My heart in secret bleeds with tender thought;
In vain it courts the solitary shade,
By every action, every look betray'd:

The pride of generous woe disdains appeal
To hearts that unrelenting frosts congeal;
Yet sure, if right Palemon can divine,
The sense of gentle pity dwells in thine:
Yes! all his cares thy sympathy shall know,
And prove the kind companion of his woe.
"Albert thou know'st, with skill and science graced;
In humble station though by fortune placed,
Yet never seaman more serenely brave
Led Britain's conquering squadrons o'er the wave:
Where full in view Augusta's spires are seen
With flowery lawns, and waving woods between,
An humble habitation rose, beside
Where Thames meandering rolls his ample tide:
There live the hope and pleasure of his life,
A pious daughter, and a faithful wife:
For his return with fond officious care
Still every grateful object these prepare:
Whatever can allure the smell or sight,
Or wake the drooping spirits to delight.
"This blooming maid in virtue's path to guide
The admiring parents all their care applied;
Her spotless soul to soft affection train'd,
No voice untuned, no sickening folly stain'd:
Not fairer grows the lily of the vale,

Whose bosom opens to the vernal gale:
Her eyes, unconscious of their fatal charms,
Thrill'd every heart with exquisite alarms:
Her face, in beauty's sweet attraction drest,
The smile of maiden innocence exprest;
While health, that rises with the new-born day,
Breathed o'er her cheek the softest blush of May:
Still in her look complacence smiled serene;
She moved the charmer of the rural scene!
"'Twas at that season, when the fields resume
Their loveliest hues, array'd in vernal bloom:
Yon ship, rich freighted from the Italian shore,
To Thames' fair banks her costly tribute bore:
While thus my father saw his ample hoard,
From this return, with recent treasures stored;
Me, with affairs of commerce charged, he sent
To Albert's humble mansion — soon I went!
Too soon, alas! unconscious of the event.
There, struck with sweet surprise and silent awe,
The gentle mistress of my hopes I saw;
There, wounded first by love's resistless arms,
My glowing bosom throbb'd with strange alarms:
My ever charming Anna! who alone
Can all the frowns of cruel fate atone;
Oh! while all-conscious memory holds her power,
Can I forget that sweetly-painful hour,

When from those eyes, with lovely lightning
fraught,
My fluttering spirits first the infection caught?
When, as I gazed, my faltering tongue betray'd
The heart's quick tumults, or refused its aid;
While the dim light my ravish'd eyes forsook,
And every limb, unstrung with terror, shook:
With all her powers, dissenting reason strove
To tame at first the kindling flame of love:
She strove in vain; subdued by charms divine,
My soul a victim fell at beauty's shrine.
Oft from the din of bustling life I stray'd,
In happier scenes to see my lovely maid;
Full oft, where Thames his wandering current leads,
We roved at evening hour through flowery meads;
There, while my heart's soft anguish I reveal'd,
To her with tender sighs my hope appeal'd:
While the sweet nymph my faithful tale believed,
Her snowy breast with secret tumult heaved;
For, train'd in rural scenes from earliest youth,
Nature was hers, and innocence, and truth:
She never knew the city damsel's art,
Whose frothy pertness charms the vacant heart.—
My suit prevail'd! for love inform'd my tongue,
And on his votary's lips persuasion hung.
Her eyes with conscious sympathy withdrew,

And o'er her cheek the rosy current flew.
Thrice happy hours! where with no dark allay
Life's fairest sunshine gilds the vernal day:
For here the sigh, that soft affection heaves,
From stings of sharper woe the soul relieves:
Elysian scenes! too happy long to last,
Too soon a storm the smiling dawn o'ercast:
Too soon some demon to my father bore
The tidings, that his heart with anguish tore.
My pride to kindle, with dissuasive voice
Awhile he labour'd to degrade my choice:
Then, in the whirling wave of pleasure, sought
From its loved object to divert my thought:
With equal hope he might attempt to bind
In chains of adamant the lawless wind;
For love had aim'd the fatal shaft too sure,
Hope fed the wound, and absence knew no cure.
With alienated look, each art he saw
Still baffled by superior nature's law.
His anxious mind on various schemes revolved,
At last on cruel exile he resolved:
The rigorous doom was fix'd; alas! how vain
To him of tender anguish to complain:
His soul, that never love's sweet influence felt,
By social sympathy could never melt;
With stern command to Albert's charge he gave

To waft Palemon o'er the distant wave.
"The ship was laden and prepared to sail,
And only waited now the leading gale:
'T was ours, in that sad period, first to prove
The poignant torments of despairing love;
The impatient wish, that never feels repose,
Desire, that with perpetual current flows;
The fluctuating pangs of hope and fear,
Joy distant still, and sorrow ever near.
Thus, while the pangs of thought severer grew,
The western breezes inauspicious blew,
Hastening the moment of our last adieu.
The vessel parted on the falling tide,
Yet time one sacred hour to love supplied:
The night was silent, and advancing fast,
The moon o'er Thames her silver mantle cast;
Impatient hope the midnight path explored,
And led me to the nymph my soul adored.
Soon her quick footsteps struck my listening ear,
She came confest! the lovely maid drew near!
But, ah! what force of language can impart
The impetuous joy that glow'd in either heart:
O ye! whose melting hearts are form'd to prove
The trembling ecstasies of genuine love;
When, with delicious agony, the thought
Is to the verge of high delirium wrought;

Your secret sympathy alone can tell
What raptures then the throbbing bosom swell:
O'er all the nerves what tender tumults roll,
While love with sweet enchantment melts the soul.
"In transport lost, by trembling hope imprest,
The blushing virgin sunk upon my breast,
While hers congenial beat with fond alarms;
Dissolving softness! Paradise of charms!
Flash'd from our eyes, in warm transfusion flew
Our blending spirits that each other drew!
O bliss supreme! where virtue's self can melt
With joys, that guilty pleasure never felt;
Form'd to refine the thought with chaste desire,
And kindle sweet affection's purest fire.
Ah! wherefore should my hopeless love, she cries,—
While sorrow bursts with interrupting sighs,—
For ever destined to lament in vain,
Such flattering, fond ideas entertain:
My heart through scenes of fair illusion stray'd,
To joys, decreed for some superior maid.
'Tis mine abandon'd to severe distress
Still to complain, and never hope redress—
Go then, dear youth! thy father's rage atone,
And let this tortured bosom beat alone.
The hovering anger yet thou may'st appease;
Go then, dear youth! nor tempt the faithless seas.

Find out some happier maid, whose equal charms
With fortune's fairer joys, may bless thy arms:
Where, smiling o'er thee with indulgent ray,
Prosperity shall hail each new-born day:
Too well thou know'st good Albert's niggard fate
Ill fitted to sustain thy father's hate.
Go then, I charge thee by thy generous love,
That fatal to my father thus may prove;
On me alone let dark affliction fall,
Whose heart for thee will gladly suffer all.
Then haste thee hence, Palemon, ere too late,
Nor rashly hope to brave opposing fate.
"She ceased: while anguish in her angel-face
O'er all her beauties shower'd celestial grace:
Not Helen, in her bridal charms array'd,
Was half so lovely as this gentle maid.—
O soul of all my wishes! I replied,
Can that soft fabric stem affliction's tide?
Canst thou, bright pattern of exalted truth,
To sorrow doom the summer of thy youth,
And I, ingrateful! all that sweetness see
Consign'd to lasting misery for me?
Sooner this moment may the eternal doom
Palemon in the silent earth entomb;
Attest, thou moon, fair regent of the night!
Whose lustre sickens at this mournful sight:

By all the pangs divided lovers feel,
Which sweet possession only knows to heal:
By all the horrors brooding o'er the deep,
Where fate, and ruin, sad dominion keep;
Though tyrant duty o'er me threatening stands,
And claims obedience to her stern commands,
Should fortune, cruel or auspicious prove,
Her smile, or frown, shall never change my love;
My heart, that now must every joy resign,
Incapable of change, is only thine.
"Oh, cease to weep, this storm will yet decay,
And the sad clouds of sorrow melt away:
While through the rugged path of life we go,
All mortals taste the bitter draught of woe.
The famed and great, decreed to equal pain,
Full oft in splendid wretchedness complain:
For this, prosperity, with brighter ray
In smiling contrast gilds our vital day.
Thou too, sweet maid! ere twice ten months are o'er,
Shall hail Palemon to his native shore,
Where never interest shall divide us more.—
"Her struggling soul, o'erwhelm'd with tender grief,
Now found an interval of short relief:
So melts the surface of the frozen stream

Beneath the wintry sun's departing beam.
With cruel haste the shades of night withdrew,
And gave the signal of a sad adieu:
As on my neck the afflicted maiden hung,
A thousand racking doubts her spirit wrung;
She wept the terrors of the fearful wave,
Too oft, alas! the wandering lover's grave:
With soft persuasion I dispell'd her fear,
And from her cheek beguiled the falling tear.
While dying fondness languish'd in her eyes,
She pour'd her soul to heaven in suppliant sighs:
'Look down with pity, O ye powers above!
Who hear the sad complaint of bleeding love;
Ye, who the secret laws of fate explore,
Alone can tell if he returns no more;
Or if the hour of future joy remain,
Long-wish'd atonement of long-suffer'd pain,
Bid every guardian minister attend,
And from all ill the much-loved youth defend.'
With grief o'erwhelm'd we parted twice in vain,
And, urged by strong attraction, met again.
At last, by cruel fortune torn apart
While tender passion beat in either heart,
Our eyes transfix'd with agonizing look,
One sad farewell, one last embrace we took.
Forlorn of hope the lovely maid I left,

Pensive and pale, of every joy bereft:
She to her silent couch retired to weep,
Whilst I embark'd, in sadness, on the deep."
  His tale thus closed, from sympathy of grief
Palemon's bosom felt a sweet relief:
To mutual friendship thus sincerely true,
No secret wish, or fear, their bosoms knew;
In mutual hazards oft severely tried,
Nor hope, nor danger, could their love divide.
  Ye tender maids! in whose pathetic souls
Compassion's sacred stream impetuous rolls,
Whose warm affections exquisitely feel
The secret wound you tremble to reveal;
Ah! may no wanderer of the stormy main
Pour through your breasts the soft delicious bane;
May never fatal tenderness approve
The fond effusions of their ardent love:
Oh! warn'd, avoid the path that leads to woe,
Where thorns, and baneful weeds, alternate grow;
Let them severer stoic nymphs possess,
Whose stubborn passions feel no soft distress.
  Now as the youths returning o'er the plain
Approach'd the lonely margin of the main,
First, with attention roused, Arion eyed
The graceful lover, form'd in nature's pride:
His frame the happiest symmetry display'd,

And locks of waving gold his neck array'd;
In every look the Paphian graces shine,
Soft breathing o'er his cheek their bloom divine:
With lighten'd heart he smiled serenely gay,
Like young Adonis, or the son of May.
Not Cytherea from a fairer swain
Received her apple on the Trojan plain.
IV. The sun's bright orb, declining all serene,
Now glanced obliquely o'er the woodland scene:
Creation smiles around; on every spray
The warbling birds exalt their evening lay:
Blithe skipping o'er yon hill, the fleecy train
Join the deep chorus of the lowing plain;
The golden lime, and orange, there were seen
On fragrant branches of perpetual green;
The crystal streams that velvet meadows lave,
To the green ocean roll with chiding wave.
The glassy ocean hush'd forgets to roar,
But trembling murmurs on the sandy shore:
And lo! his surface lovely to behold
Glows in the west, a sea of living gold!
While, all above, a thousand liveries gay
The skies with pomp ineffable array.
Arabian sweets perfume the happy plains;
Above, beneath, around, enchantment reigns!
While glowing Vesper leads the starry train,

And night slow draws her veil o'er land and main,
Emerging clouds the azure east invade,
And wrap the lucid spheres in gradual shade;
While yet the songsters of the vocal grove,
With dying numbers tune the soul to love:
With joyful eyes the attentive master sees
The auspicious omens of an eastern breeze.
Round the charged bowl the sailors form a ring;
By turns recount the wondrous tale, or sing,
As love, or battle, hardships of the main,
Or genial wine, awake the homely strain:
Then some the watch of night alternate keep,
The rest lie buried in oblivious sleep.
Deep midnight now involves the livid skies,
When eastern breezes, yet enervate, rise:
The waning moon behind a watery shroud
Pale glimmer'd o'er the long protracted cloud;
A mighty halo round her silver throne,
With parting meteors cross'd, portentous shone:
This in the troubled sky full oft prevails,
Oft deem'd a signal of tempestuous gales.
  While young Arion sleeps, before his sight
Tumultuous swim the visions of the night:
Now, blooming Anna with her happy swain
Approach'd the sacred hymeneal fane;
Anon, tremendous lightnings flash between,

And funeral pomp, and weeping loves are seen:
Now with Palemon, up a rocky steep,
Whose summit trembles o'er the roaring deep,
With painful step he climb'd; while far above
Sweet Anna charm'd them with the voice of love:
Then sudden from the slippery height they fell,
While dreadful yawn'd, beneath, the jaws of hell.—
Amid this fearful trance, a thundering sound
He hears, and thrice the hollow decks rebound;
Upstarting from his couch on deck he sprung,
Thrice with shrill note the boatswain's whistle rung:
All hands unmoor! proclaims a boisterous cry,
All hands unmoor! the cavern'd rocks reply:
Roused from repose aloft the sailors swarm,
And with their levers soon the windlass arm:
The order given, up springing with a bound,
They fix the bars, and heave the windlass round;
At every turn the clanging pauls resound;
Up-torn reluctant from its oozy cave
The ponderous anchor rises o'er the wave.
High on the slippery masts the yards ascend,
And far abroad the canvas wings extend.
Along the glassy plain the vessel glides,
While azure radiance trembles on her sides;
The lunar rays in long reflection gleam,

With silver deluging the fluid stream.
Levant, and Thracian gales, alternate play,
Then in the Egyptian quarter die away.
A calm ensues; adjacent shores they dread,
The boats, with rowers mann'd, are sent ahead;
With cordage fasten'd to the lofty prow
Aloof to sea the stately ship they tow;
The nervous crew their sweeping oars extend,
And pealing shouts the shore of Candia rend:
Success attends their skill! the danger's o'er!
The port is doubled, and beheld no more.
  Now morn with gradual pace advanced on high,
Whitening with orient beam the twilight sky:
She comes not in refulgent pomp array'd,
But frowning stern, and wrapt in sullen shade.
Above incumbent mists, tall Ida's height,
Tremendous rock! emerges on the sight;
North-east, a league, the Isle of Standia bears,
And westward, Freschin's woody Cape appears.
  In distant angles while the transient gales
Alternate blow, they trim the flagging sails;
The drowsy air attentive to retain,
As from unnumber'd points it sweeps the main.
Now swelling stud-sails on each side extend,
Then stay-sails sidelong to the breeze ascend;
While all, to court the veering winds, are placed

With yards alternate square, and sharply braced.
The dim horizon lowering vapours shroud,
And blot the sun yet struggling in the cloud;
Thro' the wide atmosphere condensed with haze,
His glaring orb emits a sanguine blaze.
The pilots now their azimuth attend,
On which all courses, duly form'd, depend:
The compass placed to catch the rising ray,
The quadrant's shadows studious they survey;
Along the arch the gradual index slides,
While Phœbus down the vertic-circle glides;
Now seen on ocean's utmost verge to swim,
He sweeps it vibrant with his nether limb.
Thus height, and polar distance are obtain'd,
Then latitude, and declination, gain'd;
In chiliads next the analogy is sought,
And on the sinical triangle wrought:
By this magnetic variance is explored,
Just angles known, and polar truth restored.
The natives, while the ship departs their land,
Ashore with admiration gazing stand.
Majestically slow before the breeze
She moved triumphant o'er the yielding seas;
Her bottom through translucent waters shone,
White as the clouds beneath the blaze of noon;
The bending wales their contrast next display'd,

All fore and aft in polish'd jet array'd.
Britannia, riding awful on the prow,
Gazed o'er the vassal waves that roll'd below:
Where'er she moved the vassal waves were seen
To yield obsequious, and confess their queen.
The imperial trident graced her dexter hand,
Of power to rule the surge like Moses' wand;
The eternal empire of the main to keep,
And guide her squadrons o'er the trembling deep.
Her left, propitious, bore a mystic shield,
Around whose margin rolls the watery field;
There her bold genius in his floating car
O'er the wild billow hurls the storm of war:
And lo! the beasts that oft with jealous rage
In bloody combat met, from age to age,
Tamed into union, yoked in friendship's chain,
Draw his proud chariot round the vanquish'd main:
From the proud margin to the centre grew
Shelves, rocks, and whirlpools, hideous to the view.
The immortal shield from Neptune she received,
When first her head above the waters heaved;
Loose floated o'er her limbs an azure vest,
A figured scutcheon glitter'd on her breast;
There from one parent soil, for ever young,
The blooming rose and hardy thistle sprung.
Around her head an oaken wreath was seen,

Inwove with laurels of unfading green.
 Such was the sculptured prow; from van to rear
The artillery frown'd, a black tremendous tier!
Embalm'd with orient gum, above the wave
The swelling sides a yellow radiance gave.
On the broad stern, a pencil warm and bold,
That never servile rules of art controll'd,
An allegoric tale on high portray'd;
There a young hero, here a royal maid:
Fair England's genius in the youth exprest,
Her ancient foe, but now her friend confest,
The warlike nymph with fond regard survey'd;
No more his hostile frown her heart dismay'd:
His look, that once shot terror from afar,
Like young Alcides, or the god of war,
Serene as summer's evening skies she saw;
Serene, yet firm; though mild, impressing awe:
Her nervous arm, inured to toils severe,
Brandish'd the unconquer'd Caledonian spear:
The dreadful falchion of the hills she wore,
Sung to the harp in many a tale of yore,
That oft her rivers dyed with hostile gore.
Blue was her rocky shield; her piercing eye
Flash'd like the meteors of her native sky;
Her crest, high-plumed, was rough with many a scar,
And o'er her helmet gleam'd the northern star.

The warrior youth appear'd of noble frame,
The hardy offspring of some Runic dame:
Loose o'er his shoulders hung the slacken'd bow,
Renown'd in song, the terror of the foe!
The sword that oft the barbarous north defied,
The scourge of tyrants! glitter'd by his side:
Clad in refulgent arms in battle won,
The George emblazon'd on his corselet shone;
Fast by his side was seen a golden lyre,
Pregnant with numbers of eternal fire;
Whose strings unlock the witches' midnight spell,
Or waft rapt fancy through the gulfs of hell:
Struck with contagion, kindling fancy hears
The songs of heaven, the music of the spheres!
Borne on Newtonian wing through air she flies,
Where other suns to other systems rise.
These front the scene conspicuous; overhead
Albion's proud oak his filial branches spread:
While on the sea-beat shore obsequious stood,
Beneath their feet, the father of the flood:
Here, the bold native of her cliffs above,
Perch'd by the martial maid the bird of Jove;
There, on the watch, sagacious of his prey,
With eyes of fire, an English mastiff lay:
Yonder, fair commerce stretch'd her winged sail,
Here, frown'd the god that wakes the living gale.

High o'er the poop, the flattering winds unfurl'd
The imperial flag that rules the watery world.
Deep blushing armors all the tops invest,
And warlike trophies either quarter drest:
Then tower'd the masts, the canvas swell'd on high,
And waving streamers floated in the sky.
Thus the rich vessel moves in trim array,
Like some fair virgin on her bridal day;
Thus, like a swan, she cleaved the watery plain,
The pride and wonder of the Ægean main.

SECOND CANTO:

THE SCENE LIES AT SEA, BETWEEN CAPE FRESCHIN, IN CANDIA, AND THE ISLAND OF FALCONERA, WHICH IS NEARLY TWELVE LEAGUES NORTHWARD OF CAPE SPADO.

TIME, FROM NINE IN THE MORNING UNTIL ONE O'CLOCK OF THE NEXT DAY AT NOON.

ARGUMENT.

I. Reflections on leaving shore. II. Favourable breeze. Water-spout. The dying dolphin. Breeze freshens. Ship's rapid progress along the coast. Top-sails reefed. Gale of wind. Last appearance, bearing, and distance of Cape Spado. A squall. Top-sails double reefed. Main-sail split. The ship bears up; again hauls upon the wind. Another main-sail bent, and set. Porpoises. III. The ship driven out of her course from Candia. Heavy gale. Top-sails furled. Top-gallant-yards lowered. Heavy sea. Threatening sun-set. Difference of opinion respecting the mode of taking in the main-sail. Courses reefed. Four seamen lost off the lee main-yard-arm. Anxiety of the master, and his mates, on being near a lee-shore. Mizzen reefed. IV. A tremendous sea bursts over the deck; its consequences. The ship labours in great distress. Guns thrown overboard. Dismal appearance of the weather. Very high and dangerous sea. Storm of lightning. Severe fatigue of the crew at the pumps. Critical situation of the ship near the Island Falconera. Consultation and resolution of the officers. Speech and advice of Albert; his devout address to Heaven. Order given to scud. The fore stay-sail hoisted and split. The head yards braced aback. The mizzen-mast cut away.

THE SHIPWRECK.

CANTO II.

I. Adieu! ye pleasures of the sylvan scene,
Where peace, and calm contentment, dwell serene:
To me, in vain, on earth's prolific soil
With summer crown'd, the Elysian valleys smile;
To me those happier scenes no joy impart,
But tantalize with hope my aching heart:
Ye tempests! o'er my head congenial roll
To suit the mournful music of my soul;
In black progression, lo, they hover near,
Hail social horrors! like my fate severe:
Old ocean hail! beneath whose azure zone
The secret deep lies unexplored, unknown.
Approach, ye brave companions of the sea!
And fearless view this awful scene with me.
Ye native guardians of your country's laws!
Ye brave assertors of her sacred cause!
The muse invites you, judge if she depart,
Unequal, from the thorny rules of art;

In practice train'd, and conscious of her power,
She boldly moves to meet the trying hour:
Her voice attempting themes, before unknown
To music, sings distresses all her own.

II. O'er the smooth bosom of the faithless tides,
Propell'd by flattering gales, the vessel glides:
Rodmond exulting felt the auspicious wind,
And by a mystic charm its aim confined.
The thoughts of home, that o'er his fancy roll,
With trembling joy dilate Palemon's soul;
Hope lifts his heart, before whose vivid ray
Distress recedes, and danger melts away.
Tall Ida's summit now more distant grew,
And Jove's high hill was rising to the view
When on the larboard quarter they descry
A liquid column towering shoot on high;
The foaming base the angry whirlwinds sweep,
Where curling billows rouse the fearful deep:
Still round, and round, the fluid vortex flies,
Diffusing briny vapours o'er the skies.
This vast phenomenon, whose lofty head,
In heaven immersed, embracing clouds o'erspread,
In spiral motion first, as seamen deem,
Swells, when the raging whirlwind sweeps the stream.
The swift volution, and the enormous train,

Let sages versed in nature's lore explain.
The horrid apparition still draws nigh,
And white with foam the whirling billows fly.
The guns were primed; the vessel northward veers,
Till her black battery on the column bears:
The nitre fired; and, while the dreadful sound
Convulsive shook the slumbering air around,
The watery volume, trembling to the sky,
Burst down, a dreadful deluge, from on high!
The expanding ocean trembled as it fell,
And felt with swift recoil her surges swell;
But soon, this transient undulation o'er,
The sea subsides, the whirlwinds rage no more.
While southward now the increasing breezes veer,
Dark clouds incumbent on their wings appear:
Ahead they see the consecrated grove
Of Cyprus, sacred once to Cretan Jove.
The ship beneath her lofty pressure reels,
And to the freshening gale still deeper heels.
But now, beneath the lofty vessel's stern,
A shoal of sportive dolphins they discern
Beaming from burnish'd scales refulgent rays,
Till all the glowing ocean seems to blaze:
In curling wreaths they wanton on the tide,
Now bound aloft, now downward swiftly glide;
Awhile beneath the waves their tracks remain,

And burn in silver streams along the liquid plain.
Soon to the sport of death the crew repair,
Dart the long lance, or spread the baited snare.
One in redoubling mazes wheels along,
And glides unhappy near the triple prong:
Rodmond, unerring, o'er his head suspends
The barbed steel, and every turn attends;
Unerring aim'd, the missile weapon flew,
And, plunging, struck the fated victim through;
The upturning points his ponderous bulk sustain,
On deck he struggles with convulsive pain:
But while his heart the fatal javelin thrills,
And flitting life escapes in sanguine rills,
What radiant changes strike the astonish'd sight!
What glowing hues of mingled shade and light!
Not equal beauties gild the lucid west
With parting beams all o'er profusely drest,
Not lovelier colours paint the vernal dawn,
When orient dews impearl the enamell'd lawn;
Than from his sides in bright suffusion flow,
That now with gold empyreal seem to glow;
Now in pellucid sapphires meet the view,
And emulate the soft celestial hue;
Now beam a flaming crimson on the eye,
And now assume the purple's deeper dye:
But here description clouds each shining ray;

What terms of art can nature's powers display!
  The lighter sails, for summer winds and seas,
Are now dismiss'd, the straining masts to ease;
Swift on the deck the stud-sails all descend,
Which ready seamen from the yards unbend;
The boats then hoisted in are fix'd on board,
And on the deck with fastening gripes secured.
The watchful ruler of the helm no more
With fix'd attention eyes the adjacent shore,
But by the oracle of truth below,
The wondrous magnet, guides the wayward prow.
The powerful sails, with steady breezes swell'd,
Swift and more swift the yielding bark impell'd:
Across her stem the parting waters run,
As clouds, by tempests wafted, pass the sun.
Impatient thus she darts along the shore,
Till Ida's mount, and Jove's, are seen no more;
And, while aloof from Retimo she steers,
Maleca foreland full in front appears.
Wide o'er yon isthmus stands the cypress grove,
That once inclosed the hallow'd fane of Jove;
Here too, memorial of his name! is found
A tomb in marble ruins on the ground:
This gloomy tyrant, whose despotic sway
Compell'd the trembling nations to obey,
Thro' Greece for murder, rape, and incest known,

The muses raised to high Olympus' throne;
For oft, alas! their venal strains adorn
The prince, whom blushing virtue holds in scorn:
Still Rome and Greece record his endless fame,
And hence yon mountain yet retains his name.

But see! in confluence borne before the blast,
Clouds roll'd on clouds the dusky noon o'ercast:
The blackening ocean curls, the winds arise,
And the dark scud in swift succession flies.
While the swoln canvas bends the masts on high,
Low in the wave the leeward cannon lie.
The master calls, to give the ship relief,
The top-sails lower, and form a single reef!
Each lofty yard with slacken'd cordage reels;
Rattle the creaking blocks and ringing wheels.
Down the tall masts the top-sails sink amain,
Are mann'd and reef'd, then hoisted up again.
More distant grew receding Candia's shore,
And southward of the west Cape Spado bore.

Four hours the sun his high meridian throne
Had left, and o'er Atlantic regions shone;
Still blacker clouds, that all the skies invade,
Draw o'er his sullied orb a dismal shade:
A lowering squall obscures the southern sky,
Before whose sweeping breath the waters fly;
Its weight the top-sails can no more sustain —

Reef top-sails, reef! the master calls again.
The halyards and top-bow-lines soon are gone,
To clue-lines and reef-tackles next they run:
The shivering sails descend; the yards are square;
Then quick aloft the ready crew repair:
The weather-earings and the lee they past,
The reefs enroll'd, and every point made fast.
Their task above thus finished, they descend,
And vigilant the approaching squall attend:
It comes resistless! and with foaming sweep
Upturns the whitening surface of the deep:
In such a tempest, borne to deeds of death,
The wayward sisters scour the blasted heath.
The clouds, with ruin pregnant, now impend,
And storm, and cataracts, tumultuous blend.
Deep, on her side, the reeling vessel lies:
Brail up the mizzen quick! the master cries,
Man the clue-garnets! let the main-sheet fly!
It rends in thousand shivering shreds on high!
The main-sail all in streaming ruins tore,
Loud fluttering, imitates the thunder's roar:
The ship still labours in the oppressive strain,
Low bending, as if ne'er to rise again.
Bear up the helm a-weather! Rodmond cries:
Swift at the word the helm a-weather flies;
She feels its guiding power, and veers apace,

And now the fore-sail right athwart they brace:
With equal sheets restrain'd, the bellying sail
Spreads a broad concave to the sweeping gale.
While o'er the foam the ship impetuous flies,
The helm the attentive timoneer applies:
As in pursuit along the aërial way
With ardent eye the falcon marks his prey,
Each motion watches of the doubtful chase,
Obliquely wheeling through the fluid space;
So, govern'd by the steersman's glowing hands,
The regent helm her motion still commands.
But now the transient squall to leeward past,
Again she rallies to the sullen blast:
The helm to starboard moves; each shivering sail
Is sharply trimm'd to clasp the augmenting gale —
The mizzen draws; she springs aloof once more,
While the fore stay-sail balances before.
The fore-sail braced obliquely to the wind,
They near the prow the extended tack confined;
Then on the leeward sheet the seamen bend,
And haul the bow-line to the bowsprit-end:
To top-sails next they haste; the bunt-lines gone!
Through rattling blocks the clue-lines swiftly run;
The extending sheets on either side are mann'd,
Abroad they come! the fluttering sails expand;
The yards again ascend each comrade mast,

The leeches taught, the halyards are made fast,
The bow-lines haul'd, and yards to starboard braced,
And straggling ropes in pendant order placed.
  The main-sail, by the squall so lately rent,
In streaming pendants flying, is unbent:
With brails refix'd, another soon prepared,
Ascending, spreads along beneath the yard.
To each yard-arm the head-rope they extend,
And soon their earings and their robans bend.
That task perform'd, they first the braces slack,
Then to the chesstree drag the unwilling tack.
And, while the lee clue-garnet's lower'd away,
Taught aft the sheet they tally, and belay.
  Now to the north, from Afric's burning shore,
A troop of porpoises their course explore;
In curling wreaths they gambol on the tide,
Now bound aloft, now down the billow glide:
Their tracks awhile the hoary waves retain,
That burn in sparkling trails along the main —
These fleetest coursers of the finny race,
When threatening clouds the ethereal vault deface,
Their rout to leeward still sagacious form,
To shun the fury of the approaching storm.
  III. Fair Candia now no more beneath her lee
Protects the vessel from the insulting sea;
Round her broad arms impatient of control,

Roused from the secret deep, the billows roll:
Sunk were the bulwarks of the friendly shore,
And all the scene an hostile aspect wore.
The flattering wind, that late with promis'd aid
From Candia's bay the unwilling ship betray'd,
No longer fawns beneath the fair disguise,
But like a ruffian on his quarry flies:
Tost on the tide she feels the tempest blow,
And dreads the vengeance of so fell a foe —
As the proud horse with costly trappings gay,
Exulting, prances to the bloody fray;
Spurning the ground he glories in his might,
But reels tumultuous in the shock of fight:
E'en so, caparison'd in gaudy pride,
The bounding vessel dances on the tide.
 Fierce and more fierce the gathering tempest grew,
South, and by west, the threatening demon blew;
Auster's resistless force all air invades,
And every rolling wave more ample spreads:
The ship no longer can her top-sails bear;
No hopes of milder weather now appear.
Bow-lines and halyards are cast off again,
Clue-lines haul'd down, and sheets let fly amain:
Embrail'd each top-sail, and by braces squared,
The seamen climb aloft, and man each yard;

They furl'd the sails, and pointed to the wind
The yards, by rolling tackles then confined,
While o'er the ship the gallant boatswain flies;
Like a hoarse mastiff through the storm he cries,
Prompt to direct the unskilful still appears,
The expert he praises, and the timid cheers.
Now some, to strike top-gallant-yards attend,
Some, travellers up the weather-back-stays send,
At each mast-head the top-ropes others bend:
The parrels, lifts, and clue-lines soon are gone,
Topp'd and unrigg'd, they down the back-stays run;
The yards secure along the booms were laid,
And all the flying ropes aloft belay'd:
Their sails reduced, and all the rigging clear,
Awhile the crew relax from toils severe;
Awhile their spirits with fatigue opprest,
In vain expect the alternate hour of rest—
But with redoubling force the tempests blow,
And watery hills in dread succession flow:
A dismal shade o'ercasts the frowning skies,
New troubles grow; fresh difficulties rise;
No season this from duty to descend,
All hands on deck must now the storm attend.
His race perform'd, the sacred lamp of day
Now dipt in western clouds his parting ray:
His languid fires, half lost in ambient haze,

Refract along the dusk a crimson blaze;
Till deep immerged the sickening orb descends,
And cheerless night o'er heaven her reign extends:
Sad evening's hour, how different from the past!
No flaming pomp, no blushing glories cast,
No ray of friendly light is seen around;
The moon and stars in hopeless shade are drown'd.
  The ship no longer can whole courses bear,
To reef them now becomes the master's care;
The sailors, summon'd aft, all ready stand,
And man the enfolding brails at his command:
But here the doubtful officers dispute,
Till skill, and judgment, prejudice confute:
For Rodmond, to new methods still a foe,
Would first, at all events, the sheet let go;
To long-tried practice obstinately warm,
He doubts conviction, and relies on form.
This Albert and Arion disapprove,
And first to brail the tack up firmly move:
"The watchful seaman, whose sagacious eye
On sure experience may with truth rely,
Who from the reigning cause foretells the effect,
This barbarous practice ever will reject;
For, fluttering loose in air, the rigid sail
Soon flits to ruins in the furious gale;
And he, who strives the tempest to disarm,

Will never first embrail the lee yard-arm."
So Albert spoke; to windward, at his call,
Some seamen the clue-garnet stand to haul —
The tack 's eased off, while the involving clue
Between the pendent blocks ascending flew;
The sheet and weather-brace they now stand by,
The lee clue-garnet, and the bunt-lines ply:
Then, all prepared, Let go the sheet! he cries —
Loud rattling, jarring, through the blocks it flies!
Shivering at first, till by the blast impell'd;
High o'er the lee yard-arm the canvas swell'd;
By spilling lines embraced, with brails confined,
It lies at length unshaken by the wind.
The fore-sail then secured with equal care,
Again to reef the main-sail they repair;
While some above the yard o'er-haul the tye,
Below, the down-haul tackle others ply;
Jears, lifts, and brails, a seaman each attends,
And down the mast its mighty yard descends:
When lower'd sufficient they securely brace,
And fix the rolling tackle in its place;
The reef-lines and their earings now prepared,
Mounting on pliant shrouds they man the yard:
Far on the extremes appear two able hands,
For no inferior skill this task demands —
To windward, foremost, young Arion strides,

The lee yard-arm the gallant boatswain rides:
Each earing to its cringle first they bend,
The reef-band then along the yard extend;
The circling earings round the extremes entwined,
By outer and by inner turns they bind;
The reef-lines next from hand to hand received,
Through eyelet-holes and roban-legs were reeved;
The folding reefs in plaits inroll'd they lay,
Extend the worming lines, and ends belay.

Hadst thou, Arion! held the leeward post
While on the yard by mountain billows tost,
Perhaps oblivion o'er our tragic tale
Had then for ever drawn her dusky veil;
But ruling Heaven prolong'd thy vital date,
Severer ills to suffer, and relate.

For, while aloft the order those attend
To furl the main-sail, or on deck descend;
A sea, upsurging with stupendous roll,
To instant ruin seems to doom the whole:
O friends, secure your hold! Arion cries —
It comes all dreadful! down the vessel lies
Half buried sideways; while, beneath it tost,
Four seamen off the lee yard-arm are lost:
Torn with resistless fury from their hold,
In vain their struggling arms the yard enfold;
In vain to grapple flying ropes they try,

The ropes, alas! a solid gripe deny:
Prone on the midnight surge with panting breath
They cry for aid, and long contend with death;
High o'er their heads the rolling billows sweep,
And down they sink in everlasting sleep.
Bereft of power to help, their comrades see
The wretched victims die beneath the lee,
With fruitless sorrow their lost state bemoan,
Perhaps a fatal prelude to their own!
   In dark suspense on deck the pilots stand,
Nor can determine on the next command:
Though still they knew the vessel's armed side
Impenetrable to the clasping tide;
Though still the waters by no secret wound
A passage to her deep recesses found;
Surrounding evils yet they ponder o'er,
A storm, a dangerous sea, and leeward shore!
"Should they, though reef'd, again their sails extend,
Again in shivering streamers they may rend;
Or, should they stand, beneath the oppressive strain,
The down-press'd ship may never rise again;
Too late to weather now Morea's land,
And drifting fast on Athens' rocky strand." —
Thus they lament the consequence severe,
Where perils unallay'd by hope appear:

Long pondering in their minds each fear'd event,
At last to furl the courses they consent;
That done, to reef the mizzen next agree,
And try beneath it sidelong in the sea.
Now down the mast the yard they lower away,
Then jears and topping-lift secure belay;
The head, with doubling canvas fenced around,
In balance near the lofty peak they bound;
The reef enwrapp'd, the inserting knittles tied,
The halyards throt and peak are next applied —
The order given, the yard aloft they sway'd,
The brails relax'd, the extended sheet belay'd;
The helm its post forsook, and, lash'd a-lee,
Incline the wayward prow to front the sea.
IV. When sacred Orpheus on the Stygian coast,
With notes divine deplored his consort lost;
Though round him perils grew in fell array,
And fates and furies stood to bar his way;
Not more adventurous was the attempt, to move
The infernal powers with strains of heavenly love,
Than mine, in ornamental verse to dress
The harshest sounds that terms of art express:
Such arduous toil sage Dædalus endured
In mazes, self-invented, long immured,
Till genius her superior aid bestow'd,
To guide him through that intricate abode —

Thus, long imprison'd in a rugged way
Where Phœbus' daughters never aim'd to stray,
The muse, that tuned to barbarous sounds her
string,
Now spreads, like Dædalus, a bolder wing;
The verse begins in softer strains to flow,
Replete with sad variety of woe.
As yet, amid this elemental war,
Where desolation in his gloomy car
Triumphant rages round the starless void,
And fate on every billow seems to ride;
Nor toil, nor hazard, nor distress appear
To sink the seamen with unmanly fear:
Though their firm hearts no pageant-honour boast,
They scorn the wretch that trembles at his post;
Who from the face of danger strives to turn,
Indignant from the social hour they spurn:
Though now full oft they felt the raging tide
In proud rebellion climb the vessel's side;
Though every rising wave more dreadful grows,
And in succession dire the deck o'erflows;
No future ills unknown their souls appall,
They know no danger, or they scorn it all:
But e'en the generous spirits of the brave,
Subdued by toil, a friendly respite crave;
They, with severe fatigue alone opprest,

Would fain indulge an interval of rest.
Far other cares the master's mind employ,
Approaching perils all his hopes destroy:
In vain he spreads the graduated chart,
And bounds the distance by the rules of art;
Across the geometric plane expands
The compasses to circumjacent lands;
Ungrateful task! for, no asylum found,
Death yawns on every leeward shore around.—
While Albert thus, with horrid doubts dismay'd,
The geometric distances survey'd;
On deck the watchful Rodmond cries aloud,
Secure your lives! grasp every man a shroud—
Roused from his trance, he mounts with eyes aghast;
When o'er the ship, in undulation vast,
A giant surge down rushes from on high,
And fore and aft dissever'd ruins lie:
As when, Britannia's empire to maintain,
Great Hawke descends in thunder on the main,
Around the brazen voice of battle roars,
And fatal lightnings blast the hostile shores;
Beneath the storm their shatter'd navies groan;
The trembling deep recoils from zone to zone—
Thus the torn vessel felt the enormous stroke,
The boats beneath the thundering deluge broke;
Torn from their planks the cracking ring-bolts drew,

And gripes and lashings all asunder flew;
Companion, binnacle, in floating wreck,
With compasses and glasses strew'd the deck;
The balanced mizzen, rending to the head,
In fluttering fragments from its bolt-rope fled;
The sides convulsive shook on groaning beams,
And, rent with labour, yawn'd their pitchy seams.
They sound the well, and, terrible to hear!
Five feet immersed along the line appear:
At either pump they ply the clanking brake,
And, turn by turn, the ungrateful office take:
Rodmond, Arion, and Palemon here
At this sad task all diligent appear—
As some strong citadel begirt with foes
Tries long the tide of ruin to oppose,
Destruction near her spreads his black array,
And death and sorrow mark his horrid way:
Till, in some destined hour, against her wall
In tenfold rage the fatal thunders fall;
It breaks! it bursts before the cannonade!
And following hosts the shatter'd domes invade:
Her inmates long repel the hostile flood,
And shield their sacred charge in streams of blood:
So the brave mariners their pumps attend,
And help incessant, by rotation, lend;
But all in vain! for now the sounding cord,

Updrawn, an undiminish'd depth explored.
Nor this severe distress is found alone,
The ribs opprest by ponderous cannon groan;
Deep rolling from the watery volume's height,
The tortured sides seem bursting with their weight —
So reels Pelorus with convulsive throes,
When in his veins the burning earthquake glows;
Hoarse through his entrails roars the infernal flame,
And central thunders rend his groaning frame —
Accumulated mischiefs thus arise,
And fate, vindictive, all their skill defies:
For this, one remedy is only known,
From the torn ship her metal must be thrown;
Eventful task! which last distress requires,
And dread of instant death alone inspires:
For, while intent the yawning decks to ease,
Fill'd ever and anon with rushing seas,
Some fatal billow with recoiling sweep
May whirl the helpless wretches in the deep.
  No season this for counsel or delay;
Too soon the eventful moments haste away!
Here perseverance, with each help of art,
Must join the boldest efforts of the heart;
These only now their misery can relieve,
These only now a dawn of safety give.
While o'er the quivering deck from van to rear

Broad surges roll in terrible career,
Rodmond, Arion, and a chosen crew,
This office in the face of death pursue;
The wheel'd artillery o'er the deck to guide,
Rodmond descending claim'd the weather-side;
Fearless of heart the chief his orders gave,
Fronting the rude assaults of every wave —
Like some strong watch-tower nodding o'er the deep,
Whose rocky base the foaming waters sweep,
Untamed he stood; the stern aërial war
Had mark'd his honest face with many a scar;
Meanwhile Arion, traversing the waist,
The cordage of the leeward-guns unbraced,
And pointed crows beneath the metal placed.
Watching the roll, their forelocks they withdrew,
And from their beds the reeling cannon threw;
Then, from the windward battlements unbound,
Rodmond's associates wheel'd the artillery round;
Pointed with iron fangs, their bars beguile
The ponderous arms across the steep defile;
Then, hurl'd from sounding hinges o'er the side,
Thundering they plunge into the flashing tide.
  The ship, thus eased, some little respite finds
In this rude conflict of the seas and winds —
Such ease Alcides felt, when, clogg'd with gore,

The envenom'd mantle from his side he tore;
When, stung with burning pain, he strove too late
To stop the swift career of cruel fate;
Yet then his heart one ray of hope procured,
Sad harbinger of sevenfold pangs endured—
Such, and so short, the pause of woe she found!
Cimmerian darkness shades the deep around,
Save when the lightnings in terrific blaze
Deluge the cheerless gloom with horrid rays:
Above, all ether fraught with scenes of woe
With grim destruction threatens all below;
Beneath, the storm-lash'd surges furious rise,
And wave uproll'd on wave assails the skies;
With ever-floating bulwarks they surround
The ship, half swallow'd in the black profound.

With ceaseless hazard and fatigue opprest,
Dismay and anguish every heart possest;
For while, with sweeping inundation, o'er
The sea-beat ship the booming waters roar,
Displaced beneath by her capacious womb,
They rage their ancient station to resume;
By secret ambushes, their force to prove,
Through many a winding channel first they rove;
Till gathering fury, like the fever'd blood,
Through her dark veins they roll a rapid flood:
When unrelenting thus the leaks they found,

The clattering pumps with clanking strokes resound;
Around each leaping valve, by toil subdued,
The tough bull-hide must ever be renew'd:
Their sinking hearts unusual horrors chill,
And down their weary limbs thick dews distill;
No ray of light their dying hope redeems,
Pregnant with some new woe, each moment teems.
  Again the chief the instructive chart extends,
And o'er the figured plane attentive bends;
To him the motion of each orb was known,
That wheels around the sun's refulgent throne;
But here, alas! his science nought avails,
Skill droops unequal, and experience fails:
The different traverses, since twilight made,
He on the hydrographic circle laid;
Then, in the graduated arch contain'd,
The angle of lee-way, seven points, remain'd —
Her place discover'd by the rules of art,
Unusual terrors shook the master's heart,
When, on the immediate line of drift, he found
The rugged isle, with rocks and breakers bound,
Of Falconera; distant only now
Nine lessening leagues beneath the leeward bow
For, if on those destructive shallows tost,
The helpless bark with all her crew are lost;
As fatal still appears, that danger o'er,

The steep St. George, and rocky Gardalor.
With him the pilots, of their hopeless state,
In mournful consultation, long debate —
Not more perplexing doubts her chiefs appall
When some proud city verges to her fall,
While ruin glares around, and pale affright
Convenes her councils in the dead of night.
No blazon'd trophies o'er their concave spread,
Nor storied pillars raised aloft their head:
But here the queen of shade around them threw
Her dragon wing, disastrous to the view!
Dire was the scene with whirdwind, hail, and shower;
Black melancholy ruled the fearful hour:
Beneath, tremendous roll'd the flashing tide,
Where fate on every billow seem'd to ride —
Enclosed with ills, by peril unsubdued,
Great in distress the master-seaman stood!
Skill'd to command; deliberate to advise;
Expert in action; and in council wise —
Thus to his partners, by the crew unheard,
The dictates of his soul the chief referr'd:
  "Ye faithful mates! who all my troubles share,
Approved companions of your master's care!
To you, alas! 't were fruitless now to tell
Our sad distress, already known too well:
This morn with favouring gales the port we left,

Though now of every flattering hope bereft:
No skill, nor long experience could forecast
The unseen approach of this destructive blast;
These seas, where storms at various seasons blow,
No reigning winds nor certain omens know:
The hour, the occasion, all your skill demands,
A leaky ship, embay'd by dangerous lands!
Our bark no transient jeopardy surrounds,
Groaning she lies beneath unnumber'd wounds:
'T is ours the doubtful remedy to find,
To shun the fury of the seas and wind;
For in this hollow swell, with labour sore,
Her flank can bear the bursting floods no more.
One only shift, though desperate, we must try,
And that, before the boisterous storm to fly:
Then less her sides will feel the surges' power,
Which thus may soon the foundering hull devour.
'T is true, the vessel and her costly freight
To me consign'd, my orders only wait;
Yet, since the charge of every life is mine,
To equal votes our counsels I resign —
Forbid it, Heaven! that in this dreadful hour
I claim the dangerous reins of purblind power!
But should we now resolve to bear away,
Our hopeless state can suffer no delay:
Nor can we, thus bereft of every sail,

Attempt to steer obliquely on the gale;
For then, if broaching sideway to the sea,
Our dropsied ship may founder by the lee;
Vain all endeavours then to bear away,
Nor helm, nor pilot, would she more obey."
He said: the listening mates with fix'd regard
And silent reverence, his opinion heard;
Important was the question in debate,
And o'er their counsels hung impending fate:
Rodmond, in many a scene of peril tried,
Had oft the master's happier skill descried,
Yet now, the hour, the scene, the occasion known,
Perhaps with equal right preferr'd his own;
Of long experience in the naval art,
Blunt was his speech, and naked was his heart;
Alike to him each climate, and each blast,
The first in danger, in retreat the last:
Sagacious, balancing the opposed events,
From Albert his opinion thus dissents:—
"Too true the perils of the present hour,
Where toils succeeding toils our strength o'erpower!
Our bark, 'tis true, no shelter here can find,
Sore shatter'd by the ruffian seas and wind:
Yet where with safety can we dare to scud
Before this tempest, and pursuing flood?
At random driven, to present death we haste,

And one short hour perhaps may be our last:
Though Corinth's gulf extend along the lee,
To whose safe ports appears a passage free,
Yet think! this furious unremitting gale
Deprives the ship of every ruling sail;
And if before it she directly flies,
New ills enclose us and new dangers rise:
Here Falconera spreads her lurking snares,
There distant Greece her rugged shelves prepares;
Our hull, if once it strikes that iron coast,
Asunder bursts, in instant ruin lost;
Nor she alone, but with her all the crew,
Beyond relief, are doom'd to perish too:
Such mischiefs follow if we bear away;
O safer that sad refuge — to delay!
"Then of our purpose this appears the scope,
To weigh the danger with the doubtful hope:
Though sorely buffeted by every sea,
Our hull unbroken long may try a-lee;
The crew, though harass'd much with toils severe,
Still at their pumps, perceive no hazards near:
Shall we, incautious, then the danger tell,
At once their courage and their hope to quell?
Prudence forbids! this southern tempest soon
May change its quarter with the changing moon;
Its rage, though terrible, may soon subside,

Nor into mountains lash the unruly tide:
These leaks shall then decrease — the sails once more
Direct our course to some relieving shore."

Thus while he spoke, around from man to man
At either pump a hollow murmur ran:
For, while the vessel through unnumber'd chinks,
Above, below, the invading water drinks,
Sounding her depth they eyed the wetted scale,
And lo! the leaks o'er all their powers prevail:
Yet at their post, by terrors unsubdued,
They with redoubling force their task pursued.

And now the senior pilots seem'd to wait
Arion's voice, to close the dark debate:
Not o'er his vernal life the ripening sun
Had yet progressive twice ten summers run;
Slow to debate, yet eager to excel,
In thy sad school, stern Neptune! taught too well:
With lasting pain to rend his youthful heart
Dire fate in venom dipt her keenest dart;
Till his firm spirit, temper'd long to ill,
Forgot her persecuting scourge to feel:
But now the horrors, that around him roll,
Thus roused to action his rekindling soul: —

"Can we, delay'd in this tremendous tide,
A moment pause what purpose to decide?

Alas! from circling horrors thus combined,
One method of relief alone we find:
Thus water-logg'd, thus helpless to remain
Amid this hollow, how ill judged! how vain!
Our sea-breach'd vessel can no longer bear
The floods, that o'er her burst in dread career;
The labouring hull already seems half-fill'd
With water through a hundred leaks distill'd;
Thus drench'd by every wave, her riven deck,
Stript, and defenceless, floats a naked wreck;
At every pitch the o'erwhelming billows bend
Beneath their load the quivering bowsprit's end;
A fearful warning! since the masts on high
On that support with trembling hope rely;
At either pump our seamen pant for breath,
In dire dismay, anticipating death;
Still all our powers the increasing leaks defy,
We sink at sea, no shore, no haven nigh:
One dawn of hope yet breaks athwart the gloom
To light and save us from a watery tomb;
That bids us shun the death impending here,
Fly from the following blast, and shoreward steer.
"'Tis urged indeed, the fury of the gale
Precludes the help of every guiding sail;
And, driven before it on the watery waste,
To rocky shores and scenes of death we haste;

But haply Falconera we may shun,
And long to Grecian coasts is yet the run:
Less harass'd then, our scudding ship may bear
The assaulting surge repell'd upon her rear,
And since as soon that tempest may decay
When steering shoreward — wherefore thus delay?
Should we at last be driven by dire decree
Too near the fatal margin of the sea,
The hull dismasted there awhile may ride
With lengthen'd cables, on the raging tide;
Perhaps kind Heaven, with interposing power,
May curb the tempest ere that dreadful hour;
But here, ingulf'd and foundering, while we stay,
Fate hovers o'er and marks us for her prey."
  He said: Palemon saw with grief of heart
The storm prevailing o'er the pilot's art;
In silent terror and distress involved,
He heard their last alternative resolved:
High beat his bosom — with such fear subdued,
Beneath the gloom of some enchanted wood,
Oft in old time the wandering swain explored
The midnight wizards, breathing rites abhorr'd;
Trembling, approach'd their incantations fell,
And, chill'd with horror, heard the songs of hell.
Arion saw, with secret anguish moved,
The deep affliction of the friend he loved,

And all awake to friendship's genial heat
His bosom felt consenting tremors beat:
Alas! no season this for tender love,
Far hence the music of the myrtle grove —
He tried with soft persuasion's melting lore
Palemon's fainting courage to restore;
His wounded spirit heal'd with friendship's balm,
And bade each conflict of the mind be calm.
  Now had the pilots all the events revolved,
And on their final refuge thus resolved —
When, like the faithful shepherd who beholds
Some prowling wolf approach his fleecy folds,
To the brave crew, whom racking doubts perplex,
The dreadful purpose Albert thus directs:
  "Unhappy partners in a wayward fate!
Whose courage now is known perhaps too late;
Ye! who unmoved behold this angry storm
In conflict all the rolling deep deform;
Who, patient in adversity, still bear
The firmest front when greatest ills are near;
The truth, though painful, I must now reveal,
That long in vain I purposed to conceal:
Ingulf'd, all help of art we vainly try,
To weather leeward shores, alas! too nigh:
Our crazy bark no longer can abide
The seas, that thunder o'er her batter'd side;

And while the leaks a fatal warning give
That in this raging sea she cannot live,
One only refuge from despair we find —
At once to wear and scud before the wind:
Perhaps e'en then to ruin we may steer,
For rocky shores beneath our lee appear;
But that's remote, and instant death is here:
Yet there, by Heaven's assistance, we may gain
Some creek or inlet of the Grecian main;
Or, shelter'd by some rock, at anchor ride
Till with abating rage the blast subside:
But if, determined by the will of Heaven,
Our helpless bark at last ashore is driven,
These councils follow'd, from a watery grave
Our crew perhaps amid the surf may save: —
"And first, let all our axes be secured
To cut the masts and rigging from aboard;
Then to the quarters bind each plank and oar
To float between the vessel and the shore:
The longest cordage too must be convey'd
On deck, and to the weather-rails belay'd:
So they, who haply reach alive the land,
The extended lines may fasten on the strand,
Whene'er, loud thundering on the leeward shore,
While yet aloof, we hear the breakers roar:
Thus for the terrible event prepared,

Brace fore and aft to starboard every yard;
So shall our masts swim lighter on the wave,
And from the broken rocks our seamen save;
Then westward turn the stem, that every mast
May shoreward fall as from the vessel cast.
When o'er her side once more the billows bound,
Ascend the rigging till she strikes the ground;
And, when you hear aloft the dreadful shock
That strikes her bottom on some pointed rock,
The boldest of our sailors must descend
The dangerous business of the deck to tend:
Then burst the hatches off, and every stay
And every fastening laniard cut away,
Planks, gratings, booms, and rafts to leeward cast;
Then with redoubled strokes attack each mast,
That buoyant lumber may sustain you o'er
The rocky shelves and ledges to the shore:
But as your firmest succour, till the last
O cling securely on each faithful mast!
Though great the danger, and the task severe,
Yet bow not to the tyranny of fear;
If once that slavish yoke your souls subdue,
Adieu to hope! to life itself adieu!

"I know among you some have oft beheld
A bloodhound train, by rapine's lust impell'd,
On England's cruel coast impatient stand,

To rob the wanderers wreck'd upon their strand:
These, while their savage office they pursue,
Oft wound to death the helpless plunder'd crew,
Who, 'scaped from every horror of the main,
Implored their mercy, but implored in vain:
Yet dread not this, a crime to Greece unknown,
Such bloodhounds all her circling shores disown;
Who, though by barbarous tyranny oppress,
Can share affliction with the wretch distrest:
Their hearts, by cruel fate inured to grief,
Oft to the friendless stranger yield relief."

With conscious horror struck, the naval band
Detested for a while their native land;
They cursed the sleeping vengeance of the laws,
That thus forgot her guardian sailor's cause.

Meanwhile the master's voice again they heard
Whom, as with filial duty, all revered:
"No more remains — but now a trusty band
Must ever at the pumps industrious stand;
And, while with us the rest attend to wear,
Two skilful seamen to the helm repair —
And thou Eternal Power! whose awful sway
The storms revere, and roaring seas obey!
On thy supreme assistance we rely;
Thy mercy supplicate, if doom'd to die!
Perhaps this storm is sent with healing breath

From neighbouring shores to scourge disease and
death:
'Tis ours on thine unerring laws to trust,
With thee, great Lord! 'whatever is, is just.'"
He said: and, with consenting reverence fraught,
The sailors join'd his prayer in silent thought:
His intellectual eye, serenely bright,
Saw distant objects with prophetic light—
Thus in a land, that lasting wars oppress,
That groans beneath misfortune and distress;
Whose wealth to conquering armies falls a prey,
Till all her vigour, pride, and fame decay;
Some bold sagacious stateman, from the helm,
Sees desolation gathering o'er his realm;
He darts around his penetrating eyes
Where dangers grow, and hostile unions rise;
With deep attention marks the invading foe,
Eludes their wiles and frustrates every blow,
Tries his last art the tottering state to save,
Or in its ruins find a glorious grave.
Still in the yawning trough the vessel reels,
Ingulf'd beneath two fluctuating hills;
On either side they rise, tremendous scene!
A long dark melancholy vale between:
The balanced ship now forward, now behind,
Still felt the impression of the waves and wind,

And to the right and left by turns inclined;
But Albert from behind the balance drew,
And on the prow its double efforts threw.
The order now was given to bear away!
The order given, the timoneers obey:
Both stay-sail sheets to mid-ships were convey'd,
And round the foremast on each side belay'd;
Thus ready, to the halyards they apply,
They hoist! away the flitting ruins fly:
Yet Albert new resources still prepares,
Conceals his grief, and doubles all his cares.—
"Away there! lower the mizzen-yard on deck,"
He calls, "and brace the foremost yards aback!"
His great example every bosom fires,
New life rekindles and new hope inspires.
While to the helm unfaithful still she lies,
One desperate remedy at last he tries—
"Haste! with your weapons cut the shrouds and stay,
And hew at once the mizzen-mast away!"
He said: to cut the girding stay they run,
Soon on each side the sever'd shrouds are gone:
Fast by the fated pine bold Rodmond stands,
The impatient axe hung gleaming in his hands;
Brandish'd on high, it fell with dreadful sound,
The tall mast groaning felt the deadly wound;

Deep gash'd beneath, the tottering structure rings,
And crashing, thundering, o'er the quarter swings:
Thus, when some limb, convulsed with pangs of death,
Imbibes the gangrene's pestilential breath,
The experienced artist from the blood betrays
The latent venom, or its course delays;
But if the infection triumphs o'er his art,
Tainting the vital stream that warms the heart,
To stop the course of death's inflaming tides,
The infected member from the trunk divides.

THIRD CANTO:

THE SCENE IS EXTENDED FROM THAT PART OF
THE ARCHIPELAGO WHICH LIES
TEN MILES TO THE NORTHWARD OF FALCONERA,
TO CAPE COLONNA IN ATTICA.

THE TIME ABOUT SEVEN HOURS ; FROM ONE, UNTIL EIGHT IN THE MORNING.

ARGUMENT.

I. The beneficial influence of poetry in the civilization of mankind. Diffidence of the author. II. Wreck of the mizzen-mast cleared away. Ship put before the wind — labours much. Different stations of the officers. Appearance of the island of Falconera. III. Excursion to the adjacent nations of Greece renowned in antiquity. Athens. Socrates, Plato, Aristides. Solon. Corinth — its architecture. Sparta. Leonidas. Invasion by Xerxes. Lycurgus. Epaminondas. Present state of the Spartans. Arcadia. Former happiness, and fertility. Its present distress the effect of slavery. Ithaca, Ulysses, and Penelope. Argos and Mycæne. Agamemnon. Macronisi. Lemnos. Vulcan. Delos. Apollo and Diana. Troy. Sestos. Leander and Hero. Delphos. Temple of Apollo. Parnassus. The muses. IV. Subject resumed. Address to the spirits of the storm. A tempest, accompanied with rain, hail, and meteors. Darkness of the night, lightning and thunder. Daybreak. St. George's cliffs open upon them. The ship, in great danger, passes the island of St. George. V. Land of Athens appears. Helmsman struck blind by lightning. Ship laid broadside to the shore. Bowsprit, foremast, and main top-mast carried away. Albert, Rodmond, Arion, and Palemon strive to save themselves on the wreck of the foremast. The ship parts asunder. Death of Albert and Rodmond. Arion reaches the shore. Finds Palemon expiring on the beach. His dying address to Arion, who is led away by the humane natives.

THE SHIPWRECK.

CANTO III.

I. WHEN in a barbarous age, with blood defiled,
The human savage roam'd the gloomy wild;
When sullen ignorance her flag display'd,
And rapine, and revenge her voice obey'd;
Sent from the shores of light the muses came
The dark and solitary race to tame,
The war of lawless passions to control,
To melt in tender sympathy the soul;
The heart's remote recesses to explore,
And touch its springs when prose avail'd no more:
The kindling spirit caught the empyreal ray,
And glow'd congenial with the swelling lay;
Roused from the chaos of primeval night,
At once fair truth and reason sprung to light.
When great Mæonides, in rapid song,
The thundering tide of battle rolls along,

Each ravish'd bosom feels the high alarms,
And all the burning pulses beat to arms;
Hence, war's terrific glory to display,
Became the theme of every epic lay:
But when his strings with mournful magic tell
What dire distress Laertes' son befell,
The strains meandering through the maze of woe
Bid sacred sympathy the heart o'erflow;
Far through the boundless realms of thought he springs,
From earth upborne on Pegasean wings,
While distant poets, trembling as they view
His sunward flight, the dazzling track pursue;
His magic voice that rouses and delights,
Allures and guides to climb Olympian heights:
But I, alas! through scenes bewilder'd stray,
Far from the light of his unerring ray;
While, all unused the wayward path to tread,
Darkling I wander with prophetic dread;
To me in vain the bold Mæonian lyre
Awakes the numbers fraught with living fire;
Full oft indeed that mournful harp of yore
Wept the sad wanderer lost upon the shore;
'Tis true he lightly sketch'd the bold design,
But toils more joyless, more severe are mine;
Since o'er that scene his genius swiftly ran,

Subservient only to a nobler plan:
But I, perplex'd in labyrinths of art,
Anatomize, and blazon every part;
Attempt with plaintive numbers to display,
And chain the events in regular array;
Though hard the task to sing in varied strains,
When still unchanged the same sad theme remains:
O could it draw compassion's melting tear
For kindred miseries, oft beheld too near!
For kindred wretches, oft in ruin cast
On Albion's strand beneath the wintry blast;
For all the pangs, the complicated woe,
Her bravest sons, her guardian sailors know;
Then every breast should sigh at our distress —
This were the summit of my hoped success!
For this, my theme through mazes I pursue,
Which nor Mæonides, nor Maro knew.

II. Awhile the mast, in ruins dragg'd behind,
Balanced the impression of the helm and wind;
The wounded serpent agonized with pain
Thus trails his mangled volume on the plain:
But now, the wreck dissever'd from the rear,
The long reluctant prow began to veer:
While round before the enlarging wind it falls,
"Square fore and aft the yards," the master calls:
"You timoneers her motion still attend,

For on your steerage all our lives depend:
So steady! meet her! watch the curving prow,
And from the gale directly let her go."
"Starboard again!" the watchful pilot cries,
"Starboard!" the obedient timoneer replies:
Then back to port, revolving at command,
The wheel rolls swiftly through each glowing hand.
The ship no longer, foundering by the lee,
Bears on her side the invasions of the sea;
All lonely o'er the desert waste she flies,
Scourged on by surges, storms, and bursting skies:
As when inclosing harponeers assail
In Hyperborean seas the slumbering whale,
Soon as their javelins pierce his scaly side,
He groans, he darts impetuous down the tide;
And rack'd all o'er with lacerating pain,
He flies remote beneath the flood in vain —
So with resistless haste the wounded ship
Scuds from pursuing waves along the deep;
While, dash'd apart by her dividing prow,
Like burning adamant the waters glow;
Her joints forget their firm elastic tone,
Her long keel trembles, and her timbers groan:
Upheaved behind her in tremendous height
The billows frown, with fearful radiance bright;
Now quivering o'er the topmost waves she rides,

While deep beneath the enormous gulf divides;
Now launching headlong down the horrid vale,
Becalm'd she hears no more the howling gale;
Till up the dreadful height again she flies,
Trembling beneath the current of the skies:
As that rebellious angel, who, from heaven,
To regions of eternal pain was driven,
When dreadless he forsook the Stygian shore
The distant realms of Eden to explore;
Here, on sulphureous clouds sublime upheaved,
With daring wing the infernal air he cleaved;
There, in some hideous gulf descending prone,
Far in the void abrupt of night was thrown —
E'en so she climbs the briny mountain's height,
Then down the black abyss precipitates her flight:
The masts, about whose tops the whirlwinds sing,
With long vibration round her axle swing.
  To guide her wayward course amid the gloom,
The watchful pilots different posts assume:
Albert and Rodmond on the poop appear,
There to direct each guiding timoneer;
While at the bow the watch Arion keeps,
To shun what cruisers wander o'er the deeps:
Where'er he moves Palemon still attends,
As if on him his only hope depends;
While Rodmond, fearful of some neighbouring shore,

Cries, ever and anon, Look out afore!
  Thus o'er the flood four hours she scudding flew,
When Falconera's rugged cliffs they view
Faintly along the larboard bow descried,
As o'er its mountain tops the lightnings glide;
High o'er its summit, through the gloom of night,
The glimmering watch-tower casts a mournful light:
In dire amazement riveted they stand,
And hear the breakers lash the rugged strand—
But scarce perceived, when past the beam it flies,
Swift as the rapid eagle cleaves the skies:
That danger past reflects a feeble joy,
But soon returning fears their hope destroy:
As in the Atlantic Ocean, when we find
Some Alp of ice driven southward by the wind,
The sultry air all sickening pants around,
In deluges of torrid ether drown'd;
Till when the floating isle approaches nigh,
In cooling tides the aërial billows fly:
Awhile deliver'd from the scorching heat,
In gentler tides our feverish pulses beat:
Such transient pleasure, as they pass'd this strand,
A moment bade their throbbing hearts expand;
The illusive meteors of a lifeless fire,
Too soon they kindle, and too soon expire. [tongue
  III. Say, memory! thou, from whose unerring

Instructive flows the animated song,
What regions now the scudding ship surround?
Regions of old through all the world renown'd;
That, once the poet's theme, the muses' boast,
Now lie in ruins, in oblivion lost!
Did they, whose sad distress these lays deplore,
Unskill'd in Grecian, or in Roman lore,
Unconscious pass along each famous shore?
They did: for in this desert, joyless soil,
No flowers of genial science deign to smile;
Sad ocean's genius, in untimely hour,
Withers the bloom of every springing flower;
For native tempests here, with blasting breath,
Despoil, and doom the vernal buds to death;
Here fancy droops, while sullen clouds, and storm,
The generous temper of the soul deform:
Then, if among the wandering naval train,
One stripling, exiled from the Aonian plain,
Had e'er, entranced in fancy's soothing dream,
Approach'd to taste the sweet Castalian stream;
(Since those salubrious streams, with power divine,
To purer sense the soften'd soul refine)
Sure he, amid unsocial mates immured,
To learning lost, severer grief endured;
In vain might Phœbus' ray his mind inspire,
Since fate with torrents quench'd the kindling fire:

If one this pain of living death possest,
It dwelt supreme, Arion! in thy breast;
When, with Palemon, watching in the night
Beneath Pale Cynthia's melancholy light,
You oft recounted those surrounding states,
Whose glory fame with brazen tongue relates.
Immortal Athens first, in ruin spread,
Contiguous lies at Port Liono's head;
Great source of science! whose immortal name
Stands foremost in the glorious roll of fame;
Here god-like Socrates, and Plato shone,
And, firm to truth, eternal honour won;
The first in virtue's cause his life resign'd,
By Heaven pronounced the wisest of mankind;
The last proclaim'd the spark of vital fire,
The soul's fine essence, never could expire;
Here Solon dwelt, the philosophic sage
That fled Pisistratus' vindictive rage;
Just Aristides here maintain'd the cause,
Whose sacred precepts shine through Solon's laws:
Of all her towering structures, now alone
Some columns stand, with mantling weeds o'er-grown;
The wandering stranger near the port descries
A milk-white lion of stupendous size,
Of antique marble; hence the haven's name,

Unknown to modern natives whence it came.
Next, in the gulf of Engia, Corinth lies,
Whose gorgeous fabrics seem'd to strike the skies;
Whom, though by tyrant victors oft subdued,
Greece, Egypt, Rome, with admiration view'd:
Her name, for architecture long renown'd,
Spread like the foliage which her pillars crown'd;
But now, in fatal desolation laid,
Oblivion o'er it draws a dismal shade.
Then further westward, on Morea's land,
Fair Misitra! thy modern turrets stand:
Ah! who, unmoved with secret woe, can tell
That here great Lacedæmon's glory fell;
Here once she flourish'd, at whose trumpet's sound
War burst his chains, and nations shook around;
Here brave Leonidas from shore to shore
Through all Achaia bade her thunders roar:
He, when imperial Xerxes from afar
Advanced with Persia's sumless hosts to war,
Till Macedonia shrunk beneath his spear,
And Greece all shudder'd as the chief drew near;
He, at Thermopylæ's decisive plain,
Their force opposed with Sparta's glorious train;
Tall Oeta saw the tyrant's conquer'd bands
In gasping millions bleed on hostile lands:
Thus vanquish'd, haughty Asia heard thy name,

And Thebes, and Athens, sicken'd at thy fame;
Thy state, supported by Lycurgus' laws,
Gain'd, like thine arms, superlative applause;
E'en great Epaminondas strove in vain
To curb thy spirit with a Theban chain:
But ah! how low that free-born spirit now!
Thy abject sons to haughty tyrants bow;
A false, degenerate, superstitious race
Invest thy region, and its name disgrace.
  Not distant far, Arcadia's blest domains
Peloponnesus' circling shore contains:
Thrice happy soil! where, still serenely gay,
Indulgent Flora breathed perpetual May:
Where buxom Ceres bade each fertile field
Spontaneous gifts in rich profusion yield;
Then, with some rural nymph supremely blest,
While transport glow'd in each enamour'd breast,
Each faithful shepherd told his tender pain,
And sung of sylvan sports in artless strain;
Soft as the happy swain's enchanting lay
That pipes among The Shades of Endermay:
Now, sad reverse! oppression's iron hand
Enslaves her natives, and despoils her land;
In lawless rapine bred, a sanguine train,
With midnight ravage, scour the uncultured plain.
  Westward of these, beyond the Isthmus, lies

The long sought isle of Ithacus the wise;
Where fair Penelope, of him deprived,
To guard her honour endless schemes contrived:
She, only shielded by a stripling son,
Her lord Ulysses long to Ilion gone,
Each bold attempt of suitor-kings repell'd,
And undefiled her nuptial contract held;
True to her vows, and resolutely chaste,
Met arts with art, and triumphed at the last.
  Argos, in Greece forgotten and unknown,
Still seems her cruel fortune to bemoan:
Argos, whose monarch led the Grecian hosts
Across the Ægean main to Dardan coasts:
Unhappy prince! who, on a hostile shore,
Fatigue, and danger, ten long winters bore;
And when to native realms restored at last
To reap the harvest of thy labours past,
There found a perjured friend, and faithless wife,
Who sacrificed to impious lust thy life:
Fast by Arcadia stretch these desert plains,
And o'er the land a gloomy tyrant reigns.
  Next, Macronisi is adjacent seen,
Where adverse winds detain'd the Spartan queen;
For whom, in arms combined, the Grecian host,
With vengeance fired, invaded Phrygia's coast;
For whom so long they labour'd to destroy

The lofty turrets of imperial Troy;
Here driven by Juno's rage, the hapless dame,
Forlorn of heart, from ruin'd Ilion came:
The port an image bears of Parian stone,
Of ancient fabric, but of date unknown.
  Due east from this appears the immortal shore
That sacred Phœbus, and Diana bore,
Delos! through all the Ægean seas renown'd,
Whose coast the rocky Cyclades surround;
By Phœbus honour'd, and by Greece revered,
Her hallow'd groves e'en distant Persia fear'd:
But now a desert unfrequented land,
No human footstep marks the trackless sand.
  Thence to the north by Asia's western bound
Fair Lemnos stands, with rising marble crown'd;
Where, in her rage, avenging Juno hurl'd
Ill-fated Vulcan from the ethereal world:
There his eternal anvils first he rear'd;
Then, forged by Cyclopean art, appear'd
Thunders that shook the skies with dire alarms,
And form'd, by skill divine, immortal arms;
There, with this crippled wretch, the foul disgrace
And living scandal of the empyreal race,
In wedlock lived the beauteous queen of love;
Can such sensations heavenly bosoms move!
  Eastward of this appears the Dardan shore,

That once the imperial towers of Ilium bore,
Illustrious Troy! renown'd in every clime
Through the long records of succeeding time;
Who saw protecting gods from heaven descend
Full oft, thy royal bulwarks to defend:
Though chiefs unnumber'd in her cause were slain,
With fate the gods, and heroes, fought in vain!
That refuge of perfidious Helen's shame
At midnight was involved in Grecian flame;
And now, by time's deep ploughshare harrow'd o'er,
The seat of sacred Troy is found no more:
No trace of her proud fabrics now remains,
But corn, and vines, enrich her cultured plains;
Silver Scamander laves the verdant shore,
Scamander, oft o'erflow'd with hostile gore.

Not far removed from Ilion's famous land
In counter-view appears the Thracian strand,
Where beauteous Hero, from the turret's height,
Display'd her cresset each revolving night;
Whose gleam directed loved Leander o'er
The rolling Hellespont from Asia's shore:
Till in a fated hour, on Thracia's coast,
She saw her lover's lifeless body tost;
Then felt her bosom agony severe,
Her eyes, sad gazing, pour'd the incessant tear;
O'erwhelm'd with anguish, frantic with despair,

She beat her swelling breast, and tore her hair;
On dear Leander's name in vain she cried,
Then headlong plunged into the parting tide:
The exulting tide received the lovely maid,
And proudly from the strand its freight convey'd.
Far west of Thrace, beyond the Ægean main,
Remote from ocean lies the Delphic plain:
The sacred oracle of Phœbus there
High o'er the mount arose, divinely fair!
Achaian marble form'd the gorgeous pile,
August the fabric! elegant its style!
On brazen hinges turn'd the silver doors,
And chequer'd marble paved the polish'd floors;
The roof, where storied tablature appear'd,
On columns of Corinthian mould was rear'd;
Of shining porphyry the shafts were framed,
And round the hollow dome bright jewels flamed:
Apollo's priests, before the holy shrine
Suppliant, pour'd forth their orisons divine;
To front the sun's declining ray 'twas placed,
With golden harps and branching laurels graced:
Around the fane, engraved by Vulcan's hand,
The sciences and arts were seen to stand;
Here Æsculapius' snake display'd his crest,
And burning glories sparkled on his breast;
While from his eye's insufferable light,

Disease and death recoil'd in headlong flight:
Of this great temple, through all time renown'd,
Sunk in oblivion, no remains are found.
  Contiguous here, with hallow'd woods o'erspread,
Renown'd Parnassus lifts its honour'd head;
There roses blossom in eternal spring,
And strains celestial feather'd warblers sing:
Apollo, here, bestows the unfading wreath;
Here zephyrs aromatic odours breathe;
They o'er Castalian plains diffuse perfume,
Where round the scene perennial laurels bloom;
Fair daughters of the sun, the sacred nine!
Here wake to ecstasy their harps divine,
Or bid the Paphian lute mellifluous play,
And tune to plaintive love the liquid lay;
Their numbers every mental storm control,
And lull to harmony the afflicted soul,
With heavenly balm the tortured breast compose,
And soothe the agony of latent woes:
The verdant shades that Helicon surround,
On rosy gales seraphic tunes resound:
Perpetual summers crown the happy hours,
Sweet as the breath that fans Elysian flowers:
Hence pleasure dances in an endless round,
And love and joy, ineffable, abound. [strains
  IV. Stop, wandering thought! methinks I feel their

Diffuse delicious languor through my veins:
Adieu, ye flowery vales, and fragrant scenes,
Delightful bowers, and ever vernal greens!
Adieu, ye streams! that o'er enchanted ground
In lucid maze the Aonian hill surround;
Ye fairy scenes! where fancy loves to dwell,
And young delight, for ever, oh! farewell!
The soul with tender luxury you fill,
And o'er the sense Lethean dews distill—
Awake, O memory! from the inglorious dream,
With brazen lungs resume the kindling theme;
Collect thy powers, arouse thy vital fire,
Ye spirits of the storm my verse inspire!
Hoarse as the whirlwinds that enrage the main,
In torrent pour along the swelling strain.
Now, through the parting wave impetuous bore,
The scudding vessel stemm'd the Athenian shore;
The pilots, as the waves behind her swell,
Still with the wheeling stern their force repell;
For this assault should either quarter feel,
Again to flank the tempest she might reel:
The steersmen every bidden turn apply,
To right, and left, the spokes alternate fly—
Thus, when some conquer'd host retreats in fear,
The bravest leaders guard the broken rear;
Indignant they retire, and long oppose

Superior armies that around them close;
Still shield the flanks, the routed squadrons join,
And guide the flight in one continued line:
Thus they direct the flying bark before
The impelling floods, that lash her to the shore:
High o'er the poop the audacious seas aspire,
Uproll'd in hills of fluctuating fire;
With labouring throes she rolls on either side,
And dips her gunnels in the yawning tide;
Her joints unhinged in palsied languors play,
As ice-flakes part beneath the noon-tide ray:
The gale howls doleful thro' the blocks and shrouds,
And big rain pours a deluge from the clouds;
From wintry magazines that sweep the sky,
Descending globes of hail impetuous fly;
High on the masts, with pale and livid rays,
Amid the gloom portentous meteors blaze;
The ethereal dome in mournful pomp array'd
Now buried lies beneath impervious shade,
Now, flashing round intolerable light,
Redoubles all the horror of the night—
Such terror Sinai's trembling hill o'erspread,
When heaven's loud trumpet sounded o'er its head:
It seem'd, the wrathful angel of the wind
Had all the horrors of the skies combined,
And here, to one ill-fated ship opposed,

At once the dreadful magazine disclosed:
And lo! tremendous o'er the deep he springs,
The inflaming sulphur flashing from his wings;
Hark! his strong voice the dismal silence breaks,
Mad chaos from the chains of death awakes:
Loud, and more loud, the rolling peals enlarge,
And blue on deck the fiery tides discharge;
There all aghast the shivering wretches stood,
While chill suspense and fear congeal'd their blood;
Wide bursts in dazzling sheets the living flame,
And dread concussion rends the ethereal frame;
Sick earth convulsive groans from shore to shore,
And nature, shuddering, feels the horrid roar.

Still the sad prospect rises on my sight,
Reveal'd in all its mournful shade and light;
E'en now my ear with quick vibration feels
The explosion burst in strong rebounding peals;
Swift through my pulses glides the kindling fire,
As lightning glances on the electric wire:
Yet ah! the languid colours vainly strive
To bid the scene in native hues revive.

But lo! at last, from tenfold darkness born,
Forth issues o'er the wave the weeping morn:
Hail, sacred vision! who, on orient wings,
The cheering dawn of light propitious brings;
All nature smiling hail'd the vivid ray

That gave her beauties to returning day,
All but our ship! which, groaning on the tide,
No kind relief, no gleam of hope descried;
For now in front her trembling inmates see
The hills of Greece emerging on the lee —
So the lost lover views that fatal morn,
On which, for ever from his bosom torn,
The maid adored resigns her blooming charms,
To bless with love some happier rival's arms;
So to Eliza dawn'd that cruel day
That tore Æneas from her sight away,
That saw him parting never to return,
Herself in funeral flames decreed to burn.
O yet in clouds, thou genial source of light!
Conceal thy radiant glories from our sight;
Go, with thy smile adorn the happy plain,
And gild the scenes where health and pleasure reign:
But let not here, in scorn, thy wanton beam
Insult the dreadful grandeur of my theme.

While shoreward now the bounding vessel flies,
Full in her van St. George's cliffs arise;
High o'er the rest a pointed crag is seen,
That hung projecting o'er a mossy green;
Huge breakers on the larboard bow appear,
And full a-head its eastern ledges bear:
To steer more eastward Albert still commands,

And shun, if possible, the fatal strands—
Nearer and nearer now the danger grows,
And all their skill relentless fates oppose;
For while more eastward they direct the prow,
Enormous waves the quivering deck o'erflow;
While, as she wheels, unable to subdue
Her sallies, still they dread her broaching-to:
Alarming thought! for now no more a-lee
Her trembling side could bear the mountain'd sea,
And if pursuing waves she scuds before,
Headlong she runs upon the frightful shore;
A shore, where shelves and hidden rocks abound,
Where death in secret ambush lurks around:
Not half so dreadful to Æneas' eyes
The straits of Sicily were seen to rise,
When Palinurus from the helm descried
The rocks of Scylla on his eastern side,
While in the west, with hideous yawn disclosed,
His onward path Charybdis' gulf opposed;
The double danger he alternate view'd,
And cautiously his arduous track pursued:
Thus, while to right and left destruction lies,
Between the extremes the daring vessel flies:
With terrible irruption bursting o'er
The marble cliffs, tremendous surges roar;
Hoarse thro' each winding creek the tempest raves,

And hollow rocks repeat the groan of waves:
Should once the bottom strike this cruel shore,
The parting ship that instant is no more;
Nor she alone, but with her all the crew
Beyond relief are doom'd to perish too:
But haply she escapes the dreadful strand,
Tho' scarce her length in distance from the land;
Swift as the weapon quits the Scythian bow,
She cleaves the burning billows with her prow,
And forward hurrying with impetuous haste,
Borne on the tempest's wings the isle she past:
With longing eyes, and agony of mind,
The sailors view this refuge left behind;
Happy to bribe with India's richest ore
A safe accession to that barren shore —
When in the dark Peruvian mine confined,
Lost to the cheerful commerce of mankind,
The groaning captive wastes his life away,
For ever exiled from the realms of day,
Not half such pangs his bosom agonize
When up to distant light he rolls his eyes!
Where the broad sun, in his diurnal way
Imparts to all beside his vivid ray,
While, all forlorn, the victim pines in vain
For scenes he never shall possess again.

V. But now Athenian mountains they descry,

And o'er the surge Colonna frowns on high;
Where marble columns, long by time defaced,
Moss-cover'd on the lofty Cape are placed;
There rear'd by fair devotion to sustain
In elder times Tritonia's sacred fane;
The circling beach in murderous form appears,
Decisive goal of all their hopes and fears:
The seamen now in wild amazement see
The scene of ruin rise beneath their lee;
Swift from their minds elapsed all dangers past,
As dumb with terror they behold the last.
And now, while wing'd with ruin from on high,
Through the rent cloud the ragged lightnings fly,
A flash, quick glancing on the nerves of light,
Struck the pale helmsman with eternal night:
Rodmond, who heard a piteous groan behind,
Touch'd with compassion gazed upon the blind;
And, while around his sad companions crowd,
He guides the unhappy victim to the shroud:
"Hie thee aloft, my gallant friend!" he cries;
"Thy only succour on the mast relies."
The helm, bereft of half its vital force,
Now scarce subdued the wild unbridled course;
Quick to the abandon'd wheel Arion came,
The ship's tempestuous sallies to reclaim:
The vessel, while the dread event draws nigh,

Seems more impatient o'er the waves to fly;
Fate spurs her on! — Thus, issuing from afar,
Advances to the sun some blazing star,
And, as it feels attraction's kindling force,
Springs onward with accelerated course.
The moment fraught with fate approaches fast!
While thronging sailors climb each quivering mast;
The ship no longer now must stem the land,
And, Hard a starboard! is the last command:
While every suppliant voice to Heaven applies,
The prow, swift wheeling, to the westward flies;
Twelve sailors, on the fore-mast who depend,
High on the platform of the top ascend.
Fatal retreat! for, while the plunging prow
Immerges headlong in the wave below,
Down prest by watery weight the bowsprit bends,
And from above the stem deep-crashing rends:
Beneath her bow the floating ruins lie;
The fore-mast totters, unsustain'd on high;
And now the ship, forelifted by the sea,
Hurls the tall fabric backward o'er her lee;
While, in the general wreck, the faithful stay
Drags the main top-mast by the cap away:
Flung from the mast, the seamen strive in vain,
Through hostile floods, their vessel to regain;
Weak hope, alas! they buffet long the wave,

And grasp at life though sinking in the grave;
Till all exhausted, and bereft of strength,
O'erpower'd they yield to cruel fate at length;
The burying waters close around their head,
They sink! for ever number'd with the dead.

Those who remain the weather shrouds embrace,
Nor longer mourn their lost companions' case;
Transfixt with terror at the approaching doom,
Self-pity in their breasts alone has room:
Albert, and Rodmond, and Palemon, near
With young Arion, on the mast appear;
E'en they, amid the unspeakable distress,
In every look distracting thoughts confess,
In every vein the refluent blood congeals,
And every bosom mortal terror feels;
Begirt with all the horrors of the main
They view'd the adjacent shore, but view'd in vain:
Such torments in the drear abodes of hell,
Where sad despair laments with rueful yell,
Such torments agonize the damned breast,
That sees remote the mansions of the blest.

It comes! the dire catastrophe draws near,
Lash'd furious on by destiny severe:
The ship hangs hovering on the verge of death,
Hell yawns, rocks rise, and breakers roar beneath!
O yet confirm my heart, ye powers above!

This last tremendous shock of fate to prove;
The tottering frame of reason yet sustain,
Nor let this total havoc whirl my brain;
Since I, all trembling in extreme distress,
Must still the horrible result express.
  In vain, alas! the sacred shades of yore
Would arm the mind with philosophic lore;
In vain they'd teach us, at the latest breath
To smile serene amid the pangs of death:
Immortal Zeno's self would trembling see
Inexorable fate beneath the lee;
And Epictetus at the sight, in vain
Attempt his stoic firmness to retain;
Had Socrates, for godlike virtue famed,
And wisest of the sons of men proclaim'd,
Spectator of such various horrors been,
E'en he had stagger'd at this dreadful scene.
  In vain the cords and axes were prepared,
For every wave now smites the quivering yard;
High o'er the ship they throw a dreadful shade,
Then on her burst in terrible cascade;
Across the founder'd deck o'erwhelming roar,
And foaming, swelling, bound upon the shore.
Swift up the mounting billow now she flies,
Her shatter'd top half-buried in the skies;
Borne o'er a latent reef the hull impends,

Then thundering on the marble crags descends:
Her ponderous bulk the dire concussion feels,
And o'er upheaving surges wounded reels —
Again she plunges! hark! a second shock
Bilges the splitting vessel on the rock —
Down on the vale of death, with dismal cries,
The fated victims shuddering cast their eyes
In wild despair; while yet another stroke
With strong convulsion rends the solid oak:
Ah Heaven! — behold her crashing ribs divide!
She loosens, parts, and spreads in ruin o'er the tide.
Oh, were it mine with sacred Maro's art
To wake to sympathy the feeling heart,
Like him, the smooth and mournful verse to dress
In all the pomp of exquisite distress;
Then, too severely taught by cruel fate,
To share in all the perils I relate,
Then might I, with unrivall'd strains, deplore
The impervious horrors of a leeward shore.
As o'er the surf the bending main-mast hung,
Still on the rigging thirty seamen clung:
Some on a broken crag were struggling cast,
And there by oozy tangles grappled fast;
Awhile they bore the o'erwhelming billows' rage,
Unequal combat with their fate to wage;
Till all benumb'd, and feeble, they forego

Their slippery hold, and sink to shades below:
Some, from the main-yard-arm impetuous thrown
On marble ridges, die without a groan:
Three with Palemon on their skill depend,
And from the wreck on oars and rafts descend;
Now on the mountain-wave on high they ride,
Then downward plunge beneath the involving tide;
Till one, who seems in agony to strive,
The whirling breakers heave on shore alive:
The rest a speedier end of anguish knew,
And prest the stony beach — a lifeless crew!
Next, O unhappy chief! the eternal doom
Of Heaven decreed thee to the briny tomb:
What scenes of misery torment thy view!
What painful struggles of thy dying crew!
Thy perish'd hopes all buried in the flood
O'erspread with corses, red with human blood!
So pierced with anguish hoary Priam gazed,
When Troy's imperial domes in ruin blazed;
While he, severest sorrow doom'd to feel,
Expired beneath the victor's murdering steel —
Thus with his helpless partners to the last,
Sad refuge! Albert grasps the floating mast.
His soul could yet sustain this mortal blow,
But droops, alas! beneath superior woe;
For now strong nature's sympathetic chain

Tugs at his yearning heart with powerful strain:
His faithful wife, for ever doom'd to mourn
For him, alas! who never shall return,
To black adversity's approach exposed,
With want, and hardships unforeseen enclosed;
His lovely daughter, left without a friend
Her innocence to succour and defend,
By youth and indigence set forth a prey
To lawless guilt, that flatters to betray —
While these reflections rack his feeling mind,
Rodmond, who hung beside, his grasp resign'd;
And, as the tumbling waters o'er him roll'd,
His outstretch'd arms the master's legs enfold:
Sad Albert feels their dissolution near,
And strives in vain his fetter'd limbs to clear,
For death bids every clenching joint adhere:
All faint, to Heaven he throws his dying eyes,
And, Oh protect my wife and child! he cries —
The gushing streams roll back the unfinish'd sound,
He gasps! and sinks amid the vast profound.
  Five only left of all the shipwreck'd throng
Yet ride the mast which shoreward drives along;
With these Arion still his hold secures,
And all assaults of hostile waves endures:
O'er the dire prospect as for life he strives,
He looks if poor Palemon yet survives —

"Ah wnerefore, trusting to unequal art,
Didst thou, incautious! from the wreck depart?
Alas! these rocks all human skill defy;
Who strikes them once, beyond relief must die:
And now sore wounded, thou perhaps art tost
On these, or in some oozy cavern lost:"
Thus thought Arion; anxious gazing round
In vain, his eyes no more Palemon found —
The demons of destruction hover nigh,
And thick their mortal shafts commission'd fly:
When now a breaking surge, with forceful sway,
Two, next Arion, furious tears away;
Hurl'd on the crags, behold they gasp, they bleed!
And groaning, cling upon the elusive weed;
Another billow bursts in boundless roar!
Arion sinks! and memory views no more.
  Ha! total night and horror here preside,
My stunn'd ear tingles to the whizzing tide;
It is their funeral knell! and gliding near
Methinks the phantoms of the dead appear;
But lo! emerging from the watery grave
Again they float incumbent on the wave,
Again the dismal prospect opens round, —
The wreck, the shore, the dying, and the drown'd!
And see! enfeebled by repeated shocks,
Those two, who scramble on the adjacent rocks,

Their faithless hold no longer can retain,
They sink o'erwhelm'd! and never rise again.
Two with Arion yet the mast upbore,
That now above the ridges reach'd the shore;
Still trembling to descend, they downward gaze
With horror pale, and torpid with amaze:
The floods recoil! the ground appears below!
And life's faint embers now rekindling glow;
Awhile they wait the exhausted waves' retreat,
Then climb slow up the beach with hands and feet —
O Heaven! deliver'd by whose sovereign hand
Still on destruction's brink they shuddering stand,
Receive the languid incense they bestow,
That, damp with death, appears not yet to glow;
To thee each soul the warm oblation pays
With trembling ardour of unequal praise;
In every heart dismay with wonder strives,
And hope the sicken'd spark of life revives,
Her magic powers their exiled health restore,
Till horror and despair are felt no more.
Roused by the blustering tempest of the night,
A troop of Grecians mount Colonna's height;
When, gazing down with horror on the flood,
Full to their view the scene of ruin stood —
The surf with mangled bodies strew'd around,
And those yet breathing on the sea-wash'd ground:

Though lost to science and the nobler arts,
Yet nature's lore inform'd their feeling hearts;
Strait down the vale with hastening steps they hied,
The unhappy sufferers to assist, and guide.
  Meanwhile, those three escaped beneath explore
The first adventurous youth who reach'd the shore:
Panting, with eyes averted from the day,
Prone, helpless, on the tangly beach he lay —
It is Palemon! oh, what tumults roll
With hope and terror in Arion's soul;
"If yet unhurt he lives again to view
His friend, and this sole remnant of our crew,
With us to travel through this foreign zone,
And share the future good or ill unknown?"
Arion thus; but ah, sad doom of fate!
That bleeding memory sorrows to relate;
While yet afloat, on some resisting rock
His ribs were dash'd, and fractured with the shock:
Heart-piercing sight! those cheeks so late array'd
In beauty's bloom, are pale with mortal shade;
Distilling blood his lovely breast o'erspread,
And clogg'd the golden tresses of his head:
Nor yet the lungs by this pernicious stroke
Were wounded, or the vocal organs broke.
Down from his neck, with blazing gems array'd,
Thy image, lovely Anna! hung portray'd;

The unconscious figure, smiling all serene,
Suspended in a golden chain was seen:
Hadst thou, soft maiden! in this hour of woe
Beheld him writhing from the deadly blow,
What force of art, what language could express
Thine agony, thine exquisite distress?
But thou, alas! art doom'd to weep in vain
For him thine eyes shall never see again.
With dumb amazement pale, Arion gazed,
And cautiously the wounded youth upraised;
Palemon then, with equal pangs opprest,
In faltering accents thus his friend addrest:
"O rescued from destruction late so nigh,
Beneath whose fatal influence doom'd I lie;
Are we then, exiled to this last retreat
Of life, unhappy! thus decreed to meet?
Ah! how unlike what yester-morn enjoy'd,
Enchanting hopes! for ever now destroy'd;
For wounded, far beyond all healing power,
Palemon dies, and this his final hour:
By those fell breakers, where in vain I strove,
At once cut off from fortune, life, and love!
Far other scenes must soon present my sight,
That lie deep-buried yet in tenfold night—
Ah! wretched father of a wretched son,
Whom thy paternal prudence has undone;

How will remembrance of this blinded care
Bend down thy head with anguish, and despair!
Such dire effects from avarice arise,
That, deaf to nature's voice, and vainly wise,
With force severe endeavours to control
The noblest passions that inspire the soul.
But, O thou sacred power! whose law connects
The eternal chain of causes and effects,
Let not thy chastening ministers of rage
Afflict with sharp remorse his feeble age:
And you, Arion! who with these the last
Of all our crew survive the shipwreck past—
Ah! cease to mourn, those friendly tears restrain,
Nor give my dying moments keener pain!
Since heaven may soon thy wandering steps restore,
When parted hence, to England's distant shore;
Shouldst thou, the unwilling messenger of fate,
To him the tragic story first relate;
Oh! friendship's generous ardour then suppress,
Nor hint the fatal cause of my distress;
Nor let each horrid incident sustain
The lengthen'd tale to aggravate his pain:
Ah! then remember well my last request
For her who reigns for ever in my breast;
Yet let him prove a father and a friend,
The helpless maid to succour and defend—

Say, I this suit implored with parting breath,
So Heaven befriend him at his hour of death!
But, oh! to lovely Anna shouldst thou tell
What dire untimely end thy friend befell;
Draw o'er the dismal scene soft pity's veil,
And lightly touch the lamentable tale:
Say that my love, inviolably true,
No change, no diminution ever knew;
Lo! her bright image pendent on my neck
Is all Palemon rescued from the wreck;
Take it! and say, when panting in the wave
I struggled life and this alone to save.

"My soul, that fluttering hastens to be free,
Would yet a train of thoughts impart to thee,
But strives in vain; the chilling ice of death
Congeals my blood, and chokes the stream of breath;
Resign'd, she quits her comfortless abode
To course that long, unknown, eternal road —
O sacred source of ever-living light!
Conduct the weary wanderer in her flight:
Direct her onward to that peaceful shore,
Where peril, pain, and death prevail no more.

"When thou some tale of hapless love shalt hear,
That steals from pity's eye the melting tear;
Of two chaste hearts, by mutual passion join'd,

To absence, sorrow, and despair consign'd;
Oh! then, to swell the tides of social woe
That heal the afflicted bosom they o'erflow,
While memory dictates, this sad shipwreck tell,
And what distress thy wretched friend befell:
Then, while in streams of soft compassion drown'd,
The swains lament, and maidens weep around;
While lisping children, touch'd with infant fear,
With wonder gaze, and drop the unconscious tear;
Oh! then this moral bid their souls retain,
All thoughts of happiness on earth are vain!"
The last faint accents trembled on his tongue,
That now inactive to the palate clung;
His bosom heaves a mortal groan — he dies!
And shades eternal sink upon his eyes.
As thus defaced in death Palemon lay,
Arion gazed upon the lifeless clay;
Transfix'd he stood, with awful terror fill'd,
While down his cheek the silent drops distill'd:
"O ill-starr'd votary of unspotted truth!
Untimely perish'd in the bloom of youth;
Should e'er thy friend arrive on Albion's land,
He will obey, though painful, thy command;
His tongue the dreadful story shall display,
And all the horrors of this dismal day:
Disastrous day! what ruin hast thou bred,

What anguish to the living and the dead!
How hast thou left the widow all forlorn;
And ever doom'd the orphan child to mourn,
Through life's sad journey hopeless to complain:
Can sacred justice these events ordain?
But, O my soul! avoid that wondrous maze
Where reason, lost in endless error, strays;
As through this thorny vale of life we run,
Great Cause of all effects, thy will be done!"
Now had the Grecians on the beach arrived,
To aid the helpless few who yet survived:
While passing, they behold the waves o'erspread
With shatter'd rafts and corses of the dead;
Three still alive, benumb'd and faint they find,
In mournful silence on a rock reclined:
The generous natives, moved with social pain,
The feeble strangers in their arms sustain;
With pitying sighs their hapless lot deplore,
And lead them trembling from the fatal shore.

OCCASIONAL ELEGY,

IN WHICH THE PRECEDING NARRATIVE IS CONCLUDED.

THE scene of death is closed! the mournful strains
   Dissolve in dying languor on the ear;
Yet pity weeps, yet sympathy complains,
   And dumb suspense awaits o'erwhelm'd with fear:

But the sad muses with prophetic eye
   At once the future and the past explore;
Their harps oblivion's influence can defy,
   And waft the spirit to the eternal shore —

Then, O Palemon! if thy shade can hear
   The voice of friendship still lament thy doom,
Yet to the sad oblations bend thine ear,
   That rise in vocal incense o'er thy tomb:

From young Arion first the news received
   With terror, pale unhappy Anna read;
With inconsolable distress she grieved,
   And from her cheek the rose of beauty fled;

In vain, alas! the gentle virgin wept,
  Corrosive anguish nipt her vital bloom;
O'er her soft frame diseases sternly crept,
  And gave the lovely victim to the tomb:

A longer date of woe, the widow'd wife
  Her lamentable lot afflicted bore;
Yet both were rescued from the chains of life
  Before Arion reach'd his native shore!

The father unrelenting phrenzy stung,
  Untaught in virtue's school distress to bear;
Severe remorse his tortured bosom wrung,
  He languish'd, groan'd, and perish'd in despair.

Ye lost companions of distress, adieu!
  Your toils, and pains, and dangers are no more;
The tempest now shall howl unheard by you,
  While ocean smites in vain the trembling shore;

On you the blast, surcharged with rain and snow,
  In winter's dismal nights no more shall beat;
Unfelt by you the vertic sun may glow,
  And scorch the panting earth with baneful heat:

No more the joyful maid, with sprightly strain,
  Shall wake the dance to give you welcome home;

Nor hopeless love impart undying pain,
  When far from scenes of social joy you roam;

No more on yon wide watery waste you stray,
  While hunger and disease your life consume,
While parching thirst, that burns without allay
  Forbids the blasted rose of health to bloom;

No more you feel contagion's mortal breath
  That taints the realms with misery severe,
No more behold pale famine, scattering death,
  With cruel ravage desolate the year:

The thundering drum, the trumpet's swelling strain
  Unheard, shall form the long embattled line:
Unheard, the deep foundations of the main
  Shall tremble, when the hostile squadrons join:

Since grief, fatigue, and hazards still molest
  The wandering vassals of the faithless deep;
Oh! happier now escaped to endless rest,
  Than we who still survive to wake, and weep:

What though no funeral pomp, no borrow'd tear,
  Your hour of death to gazing crowds shall tell;
Nor weeping friends attend your sable bier,
  Who sadly listen to the passing bell;

The tutor'd sigh, the vain parade of woe,
  No real anguish to the soul impart;
And oft, alas! the tear that friends bestow,
  Belies the latent feelings of the heart:

What though no sculptured pile your name displays,
  Like those who perish in their country's cause;
What though no epic muse in living lays
  Records your dreadful daring with applause,—

Full oft the flattering marble bids renown
  With blazon'd trophies deck the spotted name;
And oft, too oft, the venal muses crown
  The slaves of vice with never-dying fame.

Yet shall remembrance from oblivion's veil
  Relieve your scene, and sigh with grief sincere;
And soft compassion at your tragic tale
  In silent tribute pay her kindred tear.

NOTES AND ILLUSTRATIONS.

INTRODUCTION.

Page 5, line 3. *While Albion bids,* &c.

In the third edition, the beauty of the third and fourth line has been greatly injured: —

> " While ocean hears vindictive thunders roll
> Along his trembling wave from pole to pole."

The wave of ocean cannot be said to tremble: all editions subsequent to the third, render this alteration still more improper by reading "trembling waves."

P. 5, l. 12. *Than ever trembled from the vocal string.*

In the third edition, the following unequal lines were introduced after the above passage: —

> "No pomp of battle swells the exalted strain,
> Nor gleaming arms ring dreadful on the plain;
> But o'er the scene while pale remembrance weeps,
> Fate with fell triumph rides upon the deeps."

P. 5, l. 13. *A scene from dumb oblivion to restore.*

In this passage, as in some others, the third edition claims a preference. In the second, the lines ran thus:—

"To paint a scene yet strange to epic lore,
Whose desart soil no laurel ever bore."

P. 5, l. 19. *Immortal train,* &c.

This passage is also improved in the third edition; it previously had been thus expressed:—

"Ye all recording nine! whose sacred strains
With sweet enchantment charm Elysian plains;
Whose golden trumpets, fraught with endless fame,
Arts, arms, and heroes to all space proclaim."

The two succeeding lines are very beautiful, though omitted in the third edition: I have ventured to restore them, with many others of similar merit—

"Or in lamenting elegies express
The varied pang of exquisite distress."

P. 6, l. 29. *Or listen to the enchanting voice of love.*

The whole of the beautiful passage from "If e'er with trembling hope," to "Whose vaults remurmur to the roaring wave," was added in the third edition: but an error, either of the press, or of the author, is evident in the above line, as it is generally printed:—

"Or listen, while the enchanting voice of love."

Mr. Bowles suggested the reading which I have followed: Mr. Pocock, to whose taste I am greatly indebted, rather prefers "Or listened—"

P. 6, l. 31.

The solemn cadence, the impressive tones, and the judicious contrast of imagery, "If e'er with trembling hope," &c. and "Oh! by the hollow blast that moans around," are peculiarly calculated to awake attention, and are conceived in the genuine spirit of poetic taste. There are indeed a few verbal inaccuracies in this Introduction; such as—"The trumpet's breath bids ruin smile," which perhaps would have been better expressed, "The trumpet's breath bids havoc on:" but the whole is finely worked up; and, like a grand overture, prepares the mind of the reader for what follows. W. L. B.

This remark of my friend is so just, that, in consequence of it, I was induced to print the Introduction by itself, in order to render its effect more striking. It hitherto has been printed with the Narrative, or only separated by a line; and consequently has lost much of its exquisite beauty.

P. 6, l. 32. *That sweeps the wild harp with a plaintive sound.*

The Æolian harp; see Thomson (Castle of Indolence, 40, 41). This thought, so beautifully expressed, seems not only suggested by the Æolian harp, but by the hollow sound of a southerly wind; the dread of seamen in many climates, especially in the British Channel, as it is always attended with rain, and great obscurity, which increases with the storm, and renders the coast of Ireland, England, and South Wales, a dangerous lee-shore. On land, the peasants call it a high wind, i. e. one that sounds hollow and high. Seamen know its knell; and a shift of wind may be expected to follow from the west, or N. W. which blows low, being a counter current of air, furious in the extreme; and this causes the hollow sound before the gale is felt. N. P.

The learned reader may wish to be reminded of a curious passage in Hoffman's Lexicon Universale, published upwards of 150 years ago, relative to the Æolian harp; it is cited in the Gentleman's Magazine, (vol. xxiv. p. 174,) and the following lines are added: —

" Salve, quæ fingis proprio modulamine carmen,
Salve, Memnoniam vox imitata lyram!
Dulce, O! divinumque sonas sine pollicis ictu,
Dives naturæ simplicis, artis inops!
Talia, quæ incultæ dant mellea labra puellæ,
Talia sunt faciles, quæ modulantur aves! "

P. 6, l. 41. *Ah! will they leave, &c.*

An idea somewhat similar occurs in Ariosto (C. 46, stanza 17) on the subject of the piscatorial poesy of Sannazaro: —

"Jacopo Sannazar che alle Camene
Lasciar fa i monti ed abitar le arene."

F. D.

P. 7, l. 52. *A ship-boy on the high and giddy mast!*

The passage in Shakspeare's Henry the Fourth, act the third, whence this line is taken, is always deeply impressed on a seaman's mind: —

"Wilt thou, upon the high and giddy mast,
Seal up the ship-boy's eyes, and rock his brains,
In cradle of the rude imperious surge;
And in the visitation of the winds,
Who take the ruffian billows by the top
Curling their monstrous heads, and hanging them
With deaf'ning clamours in the slippery shrouds,
That with the hurly, death itself awakes?
Canst thou, O partial sleep, give thy repose
To the wet sea-boy in an hour so rude;
And, in the calmest and the stillest night,
With all appliances and means to boot,
Deny it to a king? then happy low! lie down,
Uneasy lies the head, that wears a crown."

P. 8, l. 72. *Till o'er her crew distress and death prevail.*

In the eleven lines that succeed, I have followed the second edition: in the third, the author very inadvertently introduced the following—

"Where'er he wander'd, thus vindictive fate
Pursued his weary steps with lasting hate:
Roused by her mandate, storms of black array
Winter'd the morn of life's advancing day;
Relax'd the sinews of the living lyre,
And quench'd the kindling spark of vital fire:
Thus while forgotten, or unknown, he woos,
What hope to win the coy reluctant Muse?"

These lines strongly savour of fatalism, and are unworthy of a British mariner. The minds of our mariners, I speak from experience, with very few exceptions, always display a high sense of Christianity, and a belief in an over-ruling Providence: a truth which I have endeavoured to support, throughout the whole of a publication, which the public has honoured with attention, entitled Sermons on the Character and Professional Duties of Seamen. When Falconer published the third edition, his temper was soured by disappointment; and, in this instance, he forgot the principles of a Christian Mariner.

P. 8, l. 83. *And lo! the power that wakes the eventful song!*

I had preferred the following text, as given in the first and second editions; but, in deference to a friend, whose poetic taste has been long approved, I followed the third edition: although the repetition of light, as a rhyme, in the fourth, and thirteenth line, has certainly a bad effect. As Mr. Bowles also observes, "the epithet propitious is too tame, it should have been instant light." The passage stood thus originally—

"Thee Memory! too, the tragic tale implores,
Arise! approach! unlock thy treasured stores!"—
"She comes confest, auspicious to the sight,
O'er all my soul diffusing sacred light,
Serenely mild her look; around her head
Refulgent wreaths of azure glory spread.
Her radiant wings like Iris' flaming bow,
With various hues in rich profusion glow;
With these, along the immensity of space,
She scours the rapid, intellectual race;" &c.

P. 9, l. 100. *And hoary time from her fresh youth receives.*

The classic ideas of our unfortunate mariner in many instances resemble those of the Italian poets: thus Tasso, when speaking of memory, exclaims (C. 1, st. 36):—

"Mente degli anni e dell' oblio nemica,
Delle cose custode, e dispensiera." F. D.

P. 9, l. 113. *Full on my soul the dreadful scene display.*

This and the following line were unaccountably omitted in the third edition.

CANTO I.

P. 13, l. 1.

A ship from Egypt o'er the deep impell'd
By guiding winds, her course for Venice held.

Falconer begins his narrative with all the simplicity of the great masters, and seems to have had in view the opening of the Æneid:—

> Trojæ qui primus ab oris
> Italiam, fato profugus, Lavinaque venit
> Littora:

I have followed in the first four lines, the third edition; in the second it was thus expressed:—

> "A ship from Egypt, o'er the watery plain
> Design'd her course to Adria's rich domain;
> From fair Britannia's isle derived her name,
> And thence her crew, the slaves of Fortune, came."

I was not fond of styling seamen "the slaves of fortune!"

P. 14, l. 17. *Thrice had the sun, &c.*

How admirably, yet naturally, is the whole of what follows in this, and the next page contrived, towards engaging the attention of the reader, and leading it gradually on to the great event of the poem! I have in part preferred the text of the second edition.

P. 14, l. 21. *from shore to shore, Unwearying wafted her commercial store.*

The British merchantmen, at the time this poem was written, and for a considerable time afterwards, remained trading from port to port in the Levant, and Mediterranean, until ordered for England; when they generally loaded with silks at Leghorn.

The length of time to which these voyages were extended, probably arose from the respect paid to the British flag, and the Mediterranean pass. Any British ship, though worn and crazy, sold for a considerable sum to the Genoese, or other neighbouring states, if the pass could also accompany the ship; this traffic at last caused some complaints, and is now impracticable. The pass must be returned to the lords of the Admiralty.

Mr. Eton, in his Survey of the Turkish Empire, treats at large, On the state of the British trade to the Levant (page 448, 3d edit.) and assigns four causes for its gradual decline. 1. The rivalship of other European nations. 2. The diminution of the consumption of our manufactures in Turkey, by the impoverished state of the country. 3. Some branches of trade being got into other channels. 4. The monopoly of the Levant Company in London.

P. 15, l. 51. Candia: *The haven enter*, &c.

The harbour of Candia, though naturally a fine basin, in which ships were securely sheltered from every wind, is described by Tournefort, in 1718, as capable of receiving nothing but boats. Ships of burden keep under the isle of Dia, or Standia, to the N. E. of Candia; and consequently that was the anchorage to which Falconer alludes. All merchant vessels freighted by the Turks at Candia are obliged to sail almost empty to the ports of Dia, whither their cargoes are conveyed in boats. The French merchants have in consequence taken up their residence at Canea; but even there the harbour will only receive ships of 200 tons burden, and its mouth is exposed to all the violence of the north winds; its bottom, however, is good, except to the west of the town, where there are several rocks under water extremely dangerous. The harbour of Canea might be enlarged so as to admit the largest frigates. The chief revenue of Canea consists in olive oil. According to Tournefort, the island of Candia in the year 1699, yielded 300,000 measures of oil, which the French merchants purchased, on account of the failure of oils in Provence.

P. 15, l. 54. *Mark the fell track of desolating war.*

The revolutions of this celebrated island may thus be briefly given. It received the name of Candia from the Saracens about the year 808, when they subdued it, after being repulsed in their attempts on the islands of Sardinia and Corsica by the maritime counts whom Charlemagne appointed, under the title of Comites ad custodiendam Oram Maritimam deputati. This island was afterwards annexed to the Greek empire, either under Romanus the first in 961, or as others think, under Nicephorus Phocas in 964. When the Emperor Alexis was murdered, and Baldwin was crowned, Candia passed, in 1204, from Boniface Marquis of Montserrat to the Venetians, who had assisted in that great revolution; and from them it came to the Turks after the memorable war which lasted nearly thirty years: the siege commenced in 1646, and on the fourth of October, 1670, the Grand Vizier entered Candia; which answers to what Falconer afterwards says (page 27, l. 351).

"Where late thrice fifty thousand warriors bled:
Full twice twelve summers were yon towers assail'd."

The Venetians however retained three fortresses a considerable time afterwards — Sudæ, Grabusa, and Spina-Longæa. English merchant vessels resorted to Candia about the year 1522; since (according to Rymer's Fœdera, vol. xiii. page 766) we find that Henry VIII. then appointed Censio de Balhazari (resident on the island) for life, governor, master, protector, or consul of the English nation there.

P. 15, l. 63. *Ah! who the flight of ages can revoke?*

This idea is more forcibly expressed by Falconer than even by Metastasio: —

"L'età che viene e fugge
E non ritorna più." F. D.

P. 16, l. 74.

These eyes have seen the dull reluctant soil
A seventh year mock the weary labourer's toil.

So correct is Falconer in this description of the state of Candia, that it almost is word for word, what M. Olivier of the

National Institute has lately published: "Far from the rod of the Turks, and under the shield of their privileges, the Greeks of the islands of the Archipelago, assured of being able to enjoy, to a certain degree, the fruit of their labours, in general cultivate their fields, or apply themselves to some industry with sufficient ardour and intelligence. But in Crete, exposed incessantly to see their crops taken away from them by the Aga; to be stripped of their property by the Pacha; to be insulted, cudgelled, and robbed by every Janizary; the cultivators are never inclined to snatch from the earth, by an increase of labour, a produce which they would see pass into the hands of those whom they have so much reason to hate.

"The fields which they cultivate, planted by their ancestors when a civilized, industrious, and trading people (the Venetians) governed the island, and favoured agriculture; are running to waste from day to day: the olive tree perishes; the vine disappears; the soil is washed away by the rains; yet these unfortunate Greeks, disheartened as they are, think not of repairing the damages which time is incessantly occasioning them. There is nothing but the pressing want of living and of paying the taxes, that can induce them to gather their olives, sow their lands, and give their attention to a few bees." *Travels in the Ottoman Empire* (vol. ii. p. 242).

P. 16.

This intermixture of historical reflection is very judicious, as it relieves the uniformity of the subject: it was the result of Falconer's natural feelings, but it exhibits the master-hand of the poet's discernment. W. L. B.

P. 16, l. 86. *the sun*
Through the bright Virgin, and the Scales had run.

Virgo is that constellation of the zodiac which the sun enters about the 21st or 22d of August. Libra, the Balance, or Scales, was so named, because when the sun arrives at this constellation, which is the time of the autumnal equinox, the days and nights are equal, as if weighed in a balance. Falconer with great judgment places the sun in Scorpio; which it is conjectured was so named, since, when the sun arrives at this constellation, the heavy gales, storms, and various maladies of autumn commence. The poet accordingly mentions the sickening vapours, and approaching storms, which then prevailed.

P. 17, l. 99. *A captive fetter'd to the oar of gain.*

Falconer here appears to have confused his characters: nor could I by any reference to preceding editions correct it. Albert is throughout the poem styled the master of the ship, and, in the very next page, is represented as

> . . . . the father of his crew,
> Brave, liberal, just!

Our author therefore must here have alluded to what past in the sordid mind of Palemon's father, whom he should have more correctly styled the owner of the ship. The third edition varies from the text of the second, which I have followed, yet does not in the least remove the difficulty, but, on the contrary, rather augments it:—

> "True to his trust, when sacred honour calls,
> No brooding storm the master's soul appalls:
> The advancing season warns him to the main:
> A captive fetter'd to the oar of gain."

P. 17, l. 114. *This crowns the prosperous villain with applause.*

Falconer throughout too much displays a mind that has been soured by adversity. If the prosperous villain ever seems to be crowned with applause in this world, such applause is only deceitful and treacherous, like the calm which precedes a storm. Armstrong's idea of the magic power of gold was more correct:—

> "Riches are oft by guilt or baseness earn'd,
> Or dealt by chance to shield a lucky nave,
> Or throw a cruel sunshine on a fool."

P. 17, l. 118.

In this instance, as in many others, Falconer, or some of his friends, weakened in the third edition, the beauty and correctness of the original, viz.

> "With slaughter'd victims fills the weeping plain,
> And smooths the furrows of the treacherous main."

A plain, however bloody, cannot be said to weep; nor can gold, however powerful, smooth the furrows of the ocean.

P. 18, l. 125. *Aboard, confest the father of his crew.*

The third edition, in which many beautiful lines are added to the character of Albert, reads Abroad! which spoils the whole force of the sentence. There is also a considerable portion of single-heartedness attached to the word aboard, which, perhaps, few except seamen will duly appreciate; it showed that Albert was the same man on shore, and when walking his quarter-deck.

P. 18, l. 128. *Him science taught!*

The character, and general information of the captains, or masters of our merchantmen, are not sufficiently known: what Falconer here says of Albert, is a true portrait of the majority of them. I need not look far among this class of men to find the counterpart of Albert.

P. 19, l. 154.

Where'er in ambush lurk the fatal sands,
They claim the danger, proud of skilful bands.

In the coal trade, the course of the numerous vessels to London, lying chiefly through difficult and dangerous passages between the sands, our seamen, who are employed in that valuable nursery, are trained from the early age of nine or ten years, to heave the lead, and to take the helm; and hence their superiority in those respects over seamen who have only been on foreign voyages. It was in this school that the circumnavigator Cooke was formed. N. P.

P. 19, l. 158. *O'er bar and shelve.*

A bar is known, in hydrography, to be a mass of earth, or sand, that has been collected, by the surge of the sea, at the entrance of a river, or haven, so as to render navigation difficult, and often dangerous. A shelf, or shelve, so called from the Saxon schylf, is a name given to any dangerous shallows, sand-banks, or rocks, lying immediately under the surface of the water.

FALCONER.

P. 20, l. 175. *While tardy justice slumbers o'er her sword.*

Soon after Falconer wrote, this grievance was considerably redressed: in the year 1775, and during the month of April, John Parry, a person of fortune, was executed at Shrewsbury, for having in 1773 plundered the wreck of the ship called Charming Nancy on the coast of Anglesea. Another person of the name of Roberts was also found guilty at the same time for the like offence: they moved an arrest of judgment, and their case was referred to the Judges, who decided against them: both received sentence at the Salop assizes.—Even a few months since, some inhabitants of Whitstable in Kent were brought up to London on information that great quantities of goods had been found in their possession, saved from vessels recently wrecked: yet so common was this practice, and so universal was it become in the first commercial country in the world, that these very people were much surprised, when informed they had no right to the goods.

N. P.

To the above note, I wish to add some beautiful lines that were written by Mr. Bowles at Bamborough Castle. This very ancient castle, as he informs us, (which had been the property of the family of the Forsters, whose heiress married Lord Crewe, Bishop of Durham,) is now appropriated by the will of that pious prelate, among other benevolent purposes, to the noble one of ministering instant relief to such shipwrecked mariners as may happen to be cast on that dangerous coast; for whose preservation, and that of their vessels, every possible assistance is contrived, and is at all times ready. The whole estate is vested in the hands of trustees, one of whom, Dr. Sharp, Archdeacon of Northumberland, with an active zeal, well suited to the nature of the humane institution, makes this castle his chief residence, attending with unwearied diligence to the proper application of the charity.

"Ye holy tow'rs that shade the wave-worn steep,
Long may ye rear your aged brows sublime,
Though, hurrying silent by, relentless time
Assail you, and the winter whirlwinds sweep!
For far from blazing grandeur's crowded halls,
Here charity hath fix'd her chosen seat,
Oft listening tearful when the wild winds beat,
With hollow bodings round your ancient walls;
And pity, at the dark and stormy hour
Of midnight, when the moon is hid on high,
Keeps her lone watch upon the topmost tower,
And turns her ear to each expiring cry;
Blest if her aid some fainting wretch might save,
And snatch him cold and speechless from the wave."

P. 20, l. 192. *But what avails it to record a name.*

How very beautiful and affecting is this natural transition!
W. L. B.

P. 21, l. 202–205.

Most exquisitely touched! Forlorn of heart — condemned reluctant to the faithless sea — long farewell — and laurel grove: — every epithet has its full force. W. L. B.

P. 22, l. 226. *These, chief among the ship's conducting train.*

Conducting train is not a happy expression, but I have preferred this line as it stood in the second edition, to what was deemed an improvement in the third: —

"Such were the pilots; tutor'd to divine
The untravell'd course by geometric line."

The mates of a merchant vessel cannot be styled her pilots; and it is an error which Falconer, otherwise so correct, too often makes: there was therefore no occasion to augment instances of it.

P. 22, l. 246.

Though tremblingly alive to nature's laws,
Yet ever firm to honour's sacred cause.

After these lines, the following succeed in the second edition: —

"Thrice happy soil! had learning's vital ray
Produced its pregnant blossoms to the day:
But all the abortive beauties of his mind
A sordid father's avarice confined,

And nursed alone the mercenary art
That kills the springing roses of the heart—
But he indignant saw the golden chain
In servile bonds each generous thought restrain:
His virtue still appear'd, though wrapp'd in shade,
As stars with trembling light the clouds pervade."

P. 25, l. 321. *Recall'd to memory by the adjacent shore.*

This line is most happily introduced: at once recalling the mind to the situation of the ship, and artfully preparing the reader for the episode of Palemon's history. W. L. B.

P. 26, l. 332. *A sullen languor still the skies opprest.*

How clearly is every circumstance set before us in this description! W. L. B.

P. 26, l. 340.

On deck, beneath the shading canvas spread,
Rodmond a rueful tale of wonders read.

The character of Rodmond is here admirably preserved. It can never be sufficiently lamented that the crews of our ships are not supplied with cheap editions of such books as Robinson Crusoe, Sinbad's Narrative, Roderic Random, and some of the most interesting voyages: the perusal of such works would often tend to allay the ferment of an irritated and harassed mind. So persuaded was I, from experience, of the beneficial effect likely to result from an adoption of this idea, that I mentioned it to Lord Spencer when he presided at the board: by whom it was approved.

A passage occurs in Mickle's translation of Camoens' Lusiadas, which resembles the above description by Falconer. (Ed. 8vo. vol. ii. p. 103.)

"The weary fleet before the gentle gale
With joyful hope display'd the steady sail;
Thro' the smooth deep they plough'd the lengthening way:
Beneath the wave the purple car of day
To sable night the eastern sky resign'd,
And o'er the decks cold breathed the midnight wind.
All but the watch in warm pavilions slept,
The second watch the wonted vigils kept;
Supine their limbs, the mast supports the head,
And the broad yard-sail o'er their shoulders spread
A grateful cover from the chilly gale,
And sleep's soft dews their heavy eyes assail:
Languid, against the languid power they strive,
And sweet discourse preserves their thoughts alive:
When Leonardo, whose enamour'd thought
In every dream the plighted fair one sought,
The dews of sleep what better to remove
Than the soft, woful, pleasing tales of love?
Ill timed, alas! the brave Veloso cries,
The tales of love that melt the heart and eyes;
The dear enchantments of the fair I know,
The fearful transport, and the rapturous woe:
But with our state ill suits the grief, or joy,
Let war, let gallant war our thoughts employ!
With dangers threaten'd, let the tale inspire
The scorn of danger, and the hero's fire —
His mates with joy the brave Veloso hear,
And on the youth the speaker's toil confer:
The brave Veloso takes the word with joy,
And truth, he cries, shall these slow hours decoy —
The warlike tale adorns our nation's fame;
The Twelve of England give the noble theme."

P. 32, l. 490.

The vessel parted on the falling tide,
Yet time one sacred hour to love supplied.

The ship, which was lying at her moorings in the river Thames, is said to part, on her quitting them.

The falling tide, or tide of ebb, is thus described by Dr. Hutton:—"The sea is observed to flow for about six hours, from south towards north; the sea gradually swelling; so that, entering the mouths of rivers, it drives back the river-waters towards their heads, or springs. After a continual flux of six hours, the sea seems to rest for about a quarter of an hour; after which it begins to ebb, or retire back again, from north to south, for six hours more; in which time, the water sinking, the rivers resume their natural course. Then, after a seeming pause of a quarter of an hour, the sea again begins to flow as before: and so on alternately."

P. 32, l. 500.

The lines that follow are exquisitely conceived: but they were also beautiful, though inferior, in the second edition:—

"O all ye soft perceptions, that impart
Impetuous rapture to the fainting heart;
In life's last gloom who bid the enchanting ray
Of joy, voluptuous agonies convey!"

P. 35, l. 579. *So melts the surface of the frozen stream.*

I am in doubt whether this idea was not better expressed in the second edition:—

"So feels the frozen stream at noon of day
Awhile the parting sun's enervate ray."

P. 36, l. 588. *And from her cheek beguiled the falling tear.*

It is singular that Johnson should not have more strongly marked in his excellent dictionary, this sense of the verb beguile: thus Shakspeare in Othello:—

"And often did beguile me of my tears."

This idea was not so elegantly worded in the second edition, but the following lines were added, which ought not afterwards to have been omitted:—

"So the reviving sun exhales the showers
That fall alternate on the evolving flowers."

The whole of Palemon's interesting history was considerably embellished, and enlarged, in the third edition. In the second, Palemon, accompanied by his sordid father, joins the ship at Dover; and Anna and her mother, who both came on board whilst the vessel remained in the river to take leave of Albert, are thus introduced:—

"Fast by that dome, where from afflicting fate
The veteran sailor finds a safe retreat,
The boat prepares to waft them to the shore;
They part, alas! perhaps to meet no more:
O Muse! in silence hide the mournful scene!
Where all the pangs of sympathy convene."

What a loss has this asylum experienced by the recent death of its treasurer!

P. 37, l. 610. *Palemon's bosom felt a sweet relief.*

The four lines that follow are not in the third edition, where they have been omitted to make room for a simile; of which Falconer was too fond:—

"The hapless bird, thus, ravish'd from the skies,
Where all forlorn his loved companion flies,

In secret long bewails his cruel fate,
With fond remembrance of his winged mate;
Till grown familiar with a foreign train,
Composed at length, his sadly-warbling strain
In sweet oblivion charms the sense of pain."

This simile, as Mr. Bowles observes, is new, pathetic, and poetical; but yet, its application to Palemon is totally false, since he never grew familiar with a foreign train: with him,

"Hope fed the wound, and absence knew no cure."

P. 37, l. 616. *Compassion's sacred stream impetuous rolls.*

Our poet here employs an improper epithet to mark the character of the sacred stream of compassion; and, instead of impetuous, might have rather used unceasing, or untainted.

P. 39, l. 671. *Deep midnight now involves the livid skies.*

A passage that has wonderful accuracy and beauty. The scene begins with description, picturesque and pleasing; then a general effect of the phantasms of sleep is spread over it; it then becomes more particular, and the mind is roused by the striking contrast — All hands unmoor! Nothing can exceed the manner in which this whole scene is set before us: the weighing of the anchor, and the appearance of the vessel as she glides secure along the glassy plain. W. L. B.

No one but a seaman would have thought of the epithet livid, so expressive of the discoloured sky, of that deep black and blue which pervades its concavity at sea, previous to an easterly gale. The waning moon was thus originally introduced: —

"The pale-orb'd moon, diffusing watery rays,
Gleam'd o'er protracted clouds, and ambient haze."

During the time that I passed at sea with my ever-lamented friend Admiral Payne, I was frequently induced by that superior taste for poetry which he possessed, to observe the variations of the sublime scenery with which we were surrounded. The view by moonlight at sea is strikingly beautiful; and the dimness of its waning orb renders the different parts of a ship more grand and terrific. Thomson well described it (Summer, l. 1686) —

> " A faint erroneous ray,
> Glanced from the imperfect surfaces of things,
> Flings half an image on the straining eye."

I remember watching this effect in the Impetueux off Brest, when a ray of the moon's feeble light played undulating from the horizon to that part of the deck on which I stood. A variety of gigantic meteors appeared to pass upon the waves. The moon then seemed to struggle through a thick fleecy cloud, from which at length she rapidly emerged with fresh lustre, and gave a new character to the scene. The mid-watch had just commenced: and the hoarse voice of the boatswain's mates proclaimed the hour of night. The sound of the ship's bell was long heard in sullen vibration; whilst the following passages from Hamlet came over my memory, and gave to the whole scene an additional effect: —

BERN. 'T is now struck twelve! Get thee to bed, Francisco.

FRAN. For this relief much thanks: 't is bitter cold, and I am sick at heart.

MAR. What! has this thing appeared again to-night?

BERN. I have seen nothing.

P. 40, l. 698.

The windlass is a large cylindrical piece of timber used in merchant ships to heave up the anchors: it is furnished with strong iron pauls to prevent it from turning back by the efforts of the cable, when charged with the weight of the anchor, or strained by the violent jerking of the ship in a tempestuous sea. As the windlass is heaved about in a vertical direction, it is evident that the effort of an equal number of men acting upon it will be much more powerful than on the capstan. It requires, however, some dexterity and address to manage the handspec, or lever, to the greatest advantage; and to perform this the sailors must all rise at once upon the windlass, and, fixing their bars therein, give a sudden jerk at the same instant; in which movement they are regulated by a sort of song pronounced by one of the number. The most dexterous managers of the handspec in heaving at the windlass, are generally supposed to be the colliers of Northumberland; and of all European mariners, the Dutch are certainly the most awkward, and sluggish, in this manœuvre.

FALCONER.

P. 41, l. 710. *Levant and Thracian gales.*

Or, as in the third edition, "From east to north."

P. 41, l. 715. *The stately ship they tow.*

From the Saxon teohan. Towing is chiefly used, as in the present instance, when a ship for want of wind is forced toward the shore by the swell of the sea. FALCONER.

P. 41, l. 724. *Tall Ida's height,*
Tremendous rock! emerges on the sight;
North-east, a league, the Isle of Standia bears,
And westward, Freschin's woody cape appears.

The celebrated Mount Ida, which covers almost the middle of Candia, is thus described by Tournefort, (vol. i. p. 41). "Mount Ida is nothing but a huge overgrown, ugly, sharp-raised, bald-pated eminence; not the least shadow of a landscape, no delightful grotto, no bubbling spring, nor purling rivulet to be seen. Begging Dionysius Periegetes's pardon, as likewise his commentator's the Archbishop of Thessalonica, the praises they bestowed on this mountain seem to be strained, or at least are now past their season. Ida, according to Helladius, as cited in the Biblioth of Photius, was the common appellative of all mountains, from whence a great extent of country could be discovered: and if Suidas may be credited, all forests that afford an agreeable prospect, were called Ide, from *Ἰδειν*, to see. — The Isle of Standia, or rather Dia, has been already mentioned in a previous note, as being situated N. E. of the Port of Candia; it lies at the distance of about four leagues, and contains three harbours: the two easternmost are much esteemed. — Cape Freschin, or Freschia, is the easternmost of the two projecting points of land on the northern coast of Candia, and forms a mark for ships coming to an anchor in the road."

P. 41, l. 732.

Now swelling stud-sails on each side extend,
Then stay-sails sidelong to the breeze ascend.

1. Stud, or studding-sails, called by the French Banettes en etui, are light sails, which are extended in moderate breezes beyond the skirts of the principal sails; where they appear as wings upon the yard-arms. According to a conjecture of one of Falconer's friends, these sails seem originally to have been called steadying sails, from their tendency to keep the ship in a steady course, as also from the Saxon word sted, to assist. 2. Stay-sail; though the form of sails is so extremely different, they may all be divided into sails which have either three, or four sides: a stay-sail comes under the first class, and receives its name from a large strong rope on which it is hoisted, called a stay; employed to support the mast, by being extended from its upper end towards the fore part of the ship, as the shrouds (a range of large ropes), are extended to the right and left of the mast, and behind it. The yards of a ship are said to be square, when they hang across the ship, at right angles with the mast; and braced, when they form greater or lesser angles with the ship's length.

FALCONER.

P. 42, l. 740. *The pilots now their azimuth attend.*

The magnetical azimuth, a term which astronomers have borrowed from the Arabians, is clearly described by Johnson, as being the apparent distance of the sun from the north or south point of the compass; and this is discovered, by observing with an azimuth compass, when the sun is ten or fifteen degrees above the horizon.

P. 42, l. 759. *White as the clouds beneath the blaze of noon.*

Before the art of coppering ships' bottoms was discovered, they were painted white. The wales are the strong flanks which extend along a ship's side, at different heights, throughout her whole length, and form the curves by which a vessel appears light and graceful on the water: they are usually distinguished into the main-wale, and the channel-wale. FALCONER.

P. 46, l. 841. *Deep-blushing armors all the tops invest.*

In our largest merchantmen, the tops, or platforms, which surround the heads of the lower mast (for every ship's mast, taken in its apparent length, consists of the lower mast, the top-mast, and top-gallant mast) are fenced on the aft, or hinder side, by a rail of about three feet high, stretching across, supported by stanchions; between which a netting is usually constructed, the outside of which was formerly covered with red baize, or canvas painted red, and was called the top-armor; being a sort of blind against the enemy for the men who were there stationed. This name is now nearly lost, and the netting is always covered with black canvas.

CANTO II.

P. 50, l. 25.

Rodmond exulting felt the auspicious wind,
And by a mystic charm its aim confined.

Falconer in these lines has preserved the existence of a very old custom among seamen, particularly those of Norway, Denmark, and Sweden; which consisted in their binding a rope, with several knots tied in it, around the main-mast: this they considered as an infallible spell to secure the continuance of a favourable wind. N. P.

P. 50, l. 30.

After this line, the third edition introduces eight lines, which, in the second, follow line 36, Canto i. in the present edition.

P. 50, l. 33. *they descry*
A liquid column towering shoot on high.

All that follows is truly grand, and much superior to what Camoens wrote on the same subject! who by a strange want of taste for poetical propriety, though his genius was undoubtedly of the first order, compared the appearance of the swoln enormous volume of the water-spout, to a leech on the lips of a cow! I congratulate the public that some of the smaller, yet truly exquisite poems of this original, and great writer, have been so faithfully, and so elegantly rendered into English by Lord Strangford. It is to be wished that Camoens' master-poem, the Lusiadas, might be undertaken by one so capable of expressing its beauties in English. W. L. B.

P. 50, l. 41.

In spiral motion first, as seamen deem,
Swells, when the raging whirlwind sweeps the stream.

Notwithstanding the different accounts that have been published respecting this extraordinary meteor, some philosophers still entertain a doubt, whether the water in the first instance ascends, or descends. Falconer, like all the seamen I have ever met with, favours the first idea. The same opinion was also supported by Dr. Forster in his Voyage round the World, (vol. i. p. 191). "The water," he says, "in a space of fifty or sixty fathoms, moved towards the centre; and there rising into vapour, by the force of the whirling motion ascended in a spiral form toward the clouds. According to the opinion of Signor Beccaria, water-spouts have an electrical origin, and as a remarkable proof of this, they have been dispersed by presenting to them sharp-pointed knives, or swords. — Their form is that of a speaking-trumpet, with the wider end in the clouds; and their first appearance is in the semblance of a deep cloud, the upper part of which is white, and the lower black; they are generally seen in calm weather. The subject of water-spouts, and the ascent or descent of the water in the first instance, is discussed by Mr. Oliver, and Dr. Perkins, in the second volume of the American Philosophical Transactions: Dr. Perkins supports the latter idea, and dwells on Mr. Stuart's account of water-spouts, which also tends to support the theory of descent: Mr. Stuart's figures were drawn with the appearance of a bush round their base. Dr. Lindsay also, in several letters which he published in the Gentleman's Magazine (vols. li. liii. lv.), endeavours to establish the same theory. Some valuable remarks on this subject have appeared from Professor Wilcke of Upsal.

P. 52, l. 83. *What radiant changes strike the astonish'd sight.*

Falconer feels all the enthusiasm of the ancient poets in his description of their sacred fish, whom Ovid made the preserver of his Arion. (Fasti, lib. xi. 113.) — Our naturalists now divide this genus into three species: the dolphin, the porpoise, and the grampus. The beauty of the dying dolphin even surpasses Falconer's account of it. In the above line there is a striking similarity to an expression in a late Cambridge Tripos on Fishing, by a gentleman of Trinity College: speaking of the trout, when taken out of the water, he adds — "et leti variabilis umbra." — The appearance of the dolphin in this part of the poem has additional beauty, as the sure sign of an approaching gale.

P. 53, l. 109.

Across her stem the parting waters run,
As clouds, by tempests wafted, pass the sun.

There is peculiar beauty in these lines, which perhaps none but a seaman will feel the full force of; and it is for want of this, that hardly any painter, who has not been himself at sea, can make his ships look alive, as sailors term it, upon the waves. The outspreading of the salt foam of these parting waters, gives great variety and life to marine scenery, and adds much to the correctness of any design. A ship not only throws up the salt foam with her keel ahead, but flings it out boldly at her sides, and leaves the striated sea covered with it to a considerable distance. — And now I am upon this subject let me observe, that nothing can look more forced, or unnatural in a marine drawing, than the introduction of floating barrels, or a log of wood, on which artists are often accustomed to write their names; but the various kinds of gull, Mother Carey's Chicken, and other aquatic birds, may be introduced with considerable effect.

P. 53, l. 113. *And while aloof from Retimo she steers* —

An account of this city, with a beautiful view of it, is given by Tournefort in his Voyage to the Levant — (vol. i. p. 28). It is the third place in the island, and is governed by a bashaw under the viceroy of Canea. Retimo extends along the haven, the shore of which is covered with gardens: the citadel, that was built for its security, stands on a sharp rock stretching into the sea. Ships of war were at one time laid up in ordinary below the citadel, but at present there is scarcely depth enough for small craft. Retimo is the Rhithymna of Ptolemy. — Malacha's Foreland, Cabo Maleca, or Cape Melier, lies twelve miles N. E. of Canea; the town and island of La Suda are situated beneath this cape.

P. 54, l. 127. *But see! in confluence borne before the blast:*

I do think that neither Virgil, nor any poet, ancient or modern, has ever introduced the description of a storm, or described it so clearly, faithfully, and poetically, as Falconer has done in the following lines. W. L. B.

The gradual rising of a gale of wind, (the term by which seamen denote a storm, which is entirely banished from our naval vocabulary,) has much of the sublime. The preceding calm, which Falconer has accurately noticed, is treacherous and alarming: a watery sun-set often proclaims what may be expected; and from that moment the violence of the gale gradually steals upon the mariner: until at length — it comes resistless! — If not attended with rain, a heavy sea is soon formed; like an immense ridge, it slowly moves along in dreadful grandeur; and, rising as it were from the abyss, threatens instant destruction, as the magnitude of the immense billows is increased by their approach to the ship: when suddenly the nearest sinks beneath her keel — whilst the ship falling into a trough of the sea seems almost thrown on her beam ends: as the ship rights, the billow rushes from under her with incredible force and rapidity, and with its curling and extended ridge covers the adjacent ocean with foam.

In the second edition, these lines were differently expressed: I did not know to which a preference could be given, and therefore followed the third edition —

"But see! in confluence borne before the blast,
A rolling dusk of clouds the moon o'ercast
In dreadful length diffused; the winds arise,
And swift the scud in dark succession flies."

The scud is a name given by seamen to the lowest and lightest clouds, which are swiftly driven along the atmosphere by the winds.

P. 54, l. 132. *Low in the wave the leeward cannon lie.*

When the wind crosses a ship's course either directly, or obliquely, that side of the ship, upon which it acts, is termed the weather side; and the opposite one, which is then pressed downwards, is termed the lee side; all on one side of her is accordingly called to windward, and all on the opposite side to leeward: hence also are derived the lee cannon, the lee braces, weather braces, &c. The same term is used by Milton,

"The pilot of some small night-founded skiff,
With fixed anchor,
Moors by his side under the lee." FALCONER.

P. 54, l. 134. *Topsails, reefs, blocks.*

It may be necessary to some of my readers to inform them, that topsails are large square sails, of the second magnitude, and height; as the courses are of the first magnitude, and the lowest. — Reefs are certain divisions of the sail, which are taken in, or let out, in proportion to the increase or diminution of the wind. Blocks are what landsmen would rather term from the French word, (Poulie) pullies.

P. 54, l. 139. *More distant grew receding Candia's shore:*

Falconer with great judgment still keeps his eye on the landscape of the surrounding scenery; varying by this means the uniformity of the description, and giving it a more picturesque cast, and natural effect. W. L. B.

P. 55, l. 149, &c. *Halyards — bow-lines — clue-lines — reef-tackles — earings.*

Halyards are those ropes by which sails are hoisted, or lowered; bow-lines are ropes fastened to the outer edge of square sails in three different places, that the windward edge of the sail may be bound tight forward on a side wind, in order to keep the sail from shivering. Clue-lines are fastened to the lower corners of the square sails, for the more easy furling of them. Reef-tackles are ropes fastened to the edge of the sail, just beneath the lowest reef; and being brought down to the deck by means of two blocks, are used to facilitate the operation of reefing. Earings are small ropes employed to fasten the upper corners of the principal sails, and the extremities of the reefs, to the respective yard-arms, particularly when any sail is to be close furled. FALCONER.

Pope in one of his letters speaks very contemptuously of what he styles the tarpaulin phrase: how wonderful that this phrase, in the hands of such a master as Falconer, should have been made subservient to such an almost magical effect.

W. L. B.

P. 55, l. 151. *The shivering sails descend.*

A most striking and happy expression.

P. 55, l. 164. *Brail up the mizzen quick.*

The mizzen is a large sail bent to the mizzen mast, and is commonly reckoned one of the courses, which consist of the main-sail, fore-sail, and mizzen. As the word, brails, is a general name given to all the ropes which are employed to haul up the bottoms, lower corners, and skirts of the great sails; so the drawing them together, for the more ready operation of furling, is called brailing them up. The effect which the operation of brailing up the mizzen produces, is noticed in the last note of this canto.

P. 55, l. 165. *Man the clue-garnets, let the main-sheet fly!*

Clue-garnets are the same to the main-sail and fore-sail, which the clue-lines are to all other square-sails, and are hauled up when the sail is to be furled, or brailed. Sheets: it is necessary in this place to remark, that the sheets, which are universally mistaken by our English poets for the sails, are in reality the ropes that are used to extend the clues, or lower corners of the sails, to which they are attached. FALCONER.

P. 55, l. 166. *It rends in thousand shivering shreds on high!*

As the gale rises, Falconer's description keeps pace in grandeur. The circumstances are so rapidly, and yet so distinctly brought before us, that it is impossible not to see, to hear, to partake the anxiety; and to become, if I may thus express myself, one of the unfortunate crew. W. L. B.

P. 55, l. 171. *Bear up the helm a-weather.*

The reason for putting the helm a-weather, or to the side next the wind, is to make the ship veer before it when it blows so hard that she cannot bear her side to it any longer. Veering, or wearing, is the operation by which a ship, in changing her course from one board to the other, turns her stern to windward: the French term is, virer vent arriere. FALCONER.

P. 56, l. 176. *Spreads a broad concave to the sweeping gale.*

A new and happy image, to convey an idea of the full expanded sail. W. L. B.

The playful Titania of our immortal bard describes the same effect, though not with equal force:—

"When we have laugh'd to see the sails conceive,
And grow big-bellied with the wanton wind."
(Midsummer Night's Dream, act ii.)

One of the finest pictures ever painted by my kind friend Romney was taken from this passage.

P. 56, l. 178. *Timoneer.*

The helmsman, from the French timonnier: it is however to be lamented that our poet had not selected some more familiar term from his own language.

P. 56, l. 187. *The helm to starboard moves*—

In the third edition these lines have been altered so as entirely to destroy their beauty:—

"The helm to starboard turns; with wings inclined
The sidelong canvas clasps the faithless wind."

This could not have been done by Falconer, but by some injudicious friend who was not a seaman, and thought by this means to improve the elegance of the poem. I have often thought that Mallet, who employed our author to write for the Critical Review, introduced this and other similar alterations in the Shipwreck.

P. 56, l. 190. *While the fore stay-sail balances before:*

Called with more propriety the fore top-mast stay-sail: it is of a triangular shape, and runs upon the fore top-mast stay, over the bowsprit: it consequently has an influence on the fore part of the ship, as the mizzen has on the hinder part; and, when thus used together, they may be said to balance each other. See also the last note of this canto. FALCONER.

P. 56, l. 192. *The extended tack confined.*

The main-sail, and fore-sail of a ship, are furnished with a tack on each side, which is formed of a thick rope tapering to the end, having a knot wrought upon the largest extremity, by which it is firmly retained in the clue of the sail: by this means the tack is always fastened to windward, at the same time that the sheet extends the sail to leeward. FALCONER.

P. 56, l. 195. *the bunt-lines gone!*

Bunt-lines are ropes fastened to the bottoms of the square sails to draw them up to the yards, when the sails are brailed, or furled. FALCONER.

P. 56, l. 197. *The extending sheets on either side are mann'd:*

In the third edition, the incautious pen of some fresh-water sailor is again visible; which the reader will perceive by comparing the lines as they stand in the present edition with the following: —

"On either side below the sheets are mann'd,
Again the fluttering sails their skirts expand:
Once more the top-sails, though with humbler plume,
Mounting aloft, their ancient post resume;
Again the bow-lines, and the yards are braced,
And all the entangled cords in order placed."

The word cord is not known on board a ship, and therefore could not have been used by Falconer. — A yard is said to be braced, when it is turned about the mast horizontally, either to the right, or left; the ropes employed in this service are called the larboard and starboard braces.

P. 57, l. 205–8. *Brails, head-ropes, robands.*

Brails: a general name given to all the ropes which are employed to haul up, or brail the bottoms, and lower corners of the great sails. A rope is always attached to the edges of the sails, to strengthen, and prevent them from rending: those parts of it which are on the perpendicular or sloping edges, are called leech ropes, that, at the bottom, the foot rope, and that on the top, or upper edge, the head rope. Robands, or rope bands, are small pieces of rope, of a sufficient length to pass two or three times about the yards, in order to fix to them the upper edges of the respective great sails: the robands for this purpose are passed through the eyelet holes under the head-rope.

P. 57, l. 209.

That task perform'd, they first the braces slack,
Then to the chess-tree drag the unwilling tack.
And, while the lee clue-garnet's lower'd away,
Taught aft the sheet they tally, and belay.

The braces are here slackened, because the lee-brace confining the yard, the tack could not come down until the braces were cast off. The chess-tree, called by the French taquet d'amure, consists of a perpendicular piece of wood, fastened with iron bolts, on each side the ship: in the upper part of the chess-tree is a large hole through which the tack is passed; and when the clue, or lower corner, of the sail comes down to it, the tack is said to be aboard. — The two last lines form an extraordinary instance of that power, which our author possessed, of introducing the technical terms of navigation with singular effect into poetry. Taught, the roide of the French, and dicht of the Dutch sailors, implies the state of being extended, or stretched out.

Tally, is a word applied to the operation of hauling the sheets aft, or toward the ship's stern. To belay is to fasten.

P. 58, l. 232. *But like a ruffian on his quarry flies.*

Shakspeare uses ruffian as a verb:—

"A fuller blast ne'er shook our battlements:
If it hath ruffian'd so upon the sea,
What ribs of oak, when mountains melt on them,
Can hold the mortice?" OTHELLO.

The same word is afterwards used by our author as an adjective (page 74). Quarry is a term taken from hawking, and signifies game that is flown at by a hawk. Waller uses it, though not exactly in the same sense with Falconer:—

"They their guns discharge:
This heard some ships of ours, though out of view,
And swift as eagles to the quarry flew."

P. 58, l. 240. *The bounding vessel dances on the tide.*

The whole of this, and the preceding paragraph, were added in the third edition; and, with the exception of this line, are worthy of Falconer: he could never have inserted the word dances. The situation of the ship is justly likened to that of a war-horse; who having at first exulted, on "smelling the battle afar off, the noise of the captains, and the shouting," reels amidst the subsequent shock of the combat: had Falconer lived, he would probably have written in a subsequent edition:—

"The bounding vessel labours on the tide:"

for otherwise, even supposing the vessel to dance, the simile would not hold good; as the horse reeled, in like manner the ship rolled, or rocked, or laboured.

P. 59, l. 251.

> *They furl'd the sails and pointed to the wind*
> *The yards, by rolling tackles then confined.*

Or as in the second edition,

> "Around the sail the gaskets they convey'd,
> And rolling tackles to the cap belay'd."

The rolling tackle is an assemblage of blocks or pulleys, through which a rope is passed, until it becomes four-fold, in order to confine the yard close down to leeward when the sail is furled, that the yard may not gall the mast, from the rolling of the ship. Gaskets are platted ropes to wrap round the sails when furled.

P. 59, l. 257, &c. *Top-gallant-yards, travellers, back-stays, top-ropes, parrels, lifts, topped, booms.*

Top-gallant-yards, which are the highest ones in a ship, are sent down at the approach of a heavy gale, to ease the mast-heads. Travellers are iron rings furnished with a piece of rope, one end of which encircles the ring to which it is spliced; they are principally intended to facilitate the hoisting or lowering of the top-gallant yards; for which purpose two of them are fixed on each backstay; which are long ropes that reach on each side the ship, from the top-masts (which are the second in point of height) to the chains. Top-ropes, are employed to sway up, or lower, the top-masts, top-gallant-masts, and their respective yards. Parrels, are those bands of rope, by which the yards are fastened to the masts, so as to slide up and down when requisite; and of these there are four different sorts. Lifts, are ropes which reach from each mast-head to their respective yard-arms. A yard is said to be topped, when one end of the yard is raised higher than the other, in order to lower it on deck by means of the top-ropes. Booms, are spare masts, or yards, which are placed in store on deck, between the main and fore-mast, immediately to supply the place of any that may be carried away, or injured, by stress of weather. FALCONER.

P. 60, l. 279. *And cheerless night o'er heaven her reign extends.*

This is a most correct, and awful description of a sunset preceding a storm, or rather a heavy gale of wind, and was some years since selected by Mr. Pocock as the subject of a large oil painting; in which this artist, with a bold originality of genius, represented only the sea and sky. No vessel whatever was introduced: the effect was admirable; and may be recommended to the notice of such persons as are fond of marine scenery. The spectator in this beautiful picture is supposed to be standing in a ship, and the view that lies before him is the expanse of ocean rolling in all its grandeur, without any object to intercept the sight: whilst the sickening orb of the setting sun is enveloped in the crimson scud that tinges the dusk of the horizon.

I have a melancholy pleasure in retracing scenes, that remind me of my lost and ever to be lamented friend, Admiral Payne; and, as it serves to illustrate a passage in the poem, I trust that such remembrance will not be deemed irrelevant by the reader.

We were cruising off Ushant, in the Impetueux, during an evening at the close of October, and the dreary coast so continually present to our view, created a painful uniformity, which could only be relieved by observing the variations of the expanse that was before us. — The sun had just given its parting rays, and the last shades of day lingered on the distant waves; when a sky most sublime, and threatening, attracted all our attention, and was immediately provided against by the vigilant officers of the watch. To the verge of the horizon, except where the sun had left some portion of its departing rays, a hard, lowering, blue firmament presented itself: on this floated light yellow clouds, tinged with various hues of crimson, the never-failing harbingers of a gale. A strong vivid tint was reflected from them, on the sails and rigging of the ship, which rendered the scene more dreadful. The very calm that prevailed was portentous — the sea bird shrieked as it passed! As the tempest gradually approached, and the winds issued from the treasuries of God, the thick darkness of an autumnal night closed the whole in horrid uncertainty: —

> "It was a dismal and a fearful night;
> And on my soul hung the dull weight
> Of some intolerable fate!" COWLEY.

P. 60, l. 288. *But here the doubtful officers dispute.*

This is particulary mentioned, not because there was, or could be, any dispute at such a time between a master of a ship, and his chief mate, as the former can always command the latter; but to expose the obstinacy of a number of our veteran officers, who would rather risk any thing than forego their ancient rules, although many of them are in the highest degree equally absurd and dangerous. It is to the wonderful sagacity of these philosophers, that we owe the sea maxims of avoiding to whistle in a storm, because it will increase the wind; of whistling on the wind in a calm; of nailing horse-shoes on the mast to prevent the power of witches; of nailing a fair wind to the starboard cat-head, &c. FALCONER.

P. 61, l. 306. *The tack's eased off!*

In these lines I have followed the second edition; in the third they are somewhat different: —

> "The master said; obedient to command
> To raise the tack the ready sailors stand:
> Gradual it loosens, while the involving clue,
> Swell'd by the wind, aloft unruffling flew."

It has been already remarked, that the tack is always fastened to windward; consequently, as soon as it is cast loose, and the clue-garnet is hauled up, the weather clue of the sail immediately mounts to the yard; and this operation must be carefully performed in a storm, to prevent the sail from splitting, or being torn to pieces by shivering. FALCONER.

P. 61, l. 308. *The sheet and weather-brace they now stand by.*

To stand by any rope, is, in the language of seamen, to take hold of it. Whenever the sheet is cast off, it is necessary to pull in the weather-brace, to prevent the violent shaking of the sail.

P. 61, l. 311. *Loud rattling, jarring, through the blocks it flies!*

One of the finest, and most descriptive lines in the whole poem; the beauty of which was entirely destroyed in the third, and all the subsequent editions: —

> " Thus all prepared, Let go the sheet! he cries;
> Impetuous round the ringing wheels it flies."

P. 61, l. 314. *By spilling lines embraced—*

The spilling lines, which are only used on particular occasions in tempestuous weather, are employed to draw together, and confine the belly of the sail, when inflated by the wind over the yard. FALCONER.

P. 61, l. 319. *Below, the down-haul tackle others ply.*

The violence of the gale forcing the yard much out, it could not easily have been lowered so as to reef the sail, without the application of a tackle, consisting of an assemblage of pulleys, to haul it down on the mast: this is afterwards converted into rolling tackle, which has been already described in a note, p. 164.
FALCONER.

P. 61, l. 320.

Jears, lifts, and brails, a seaman each attends,
And down the mast its mighty yard descends.

Jears, or geers, answer the same purpose to the main-sail, fore-sail, and mizzen, as haliards do to all inferior sails. The tye, a sort of runner, or thick rope, is the upper part of the jears. The size of the main-yard, when it is gradually lowered, appears truly tremendous and mighty, as our poet terms it; I could never behold it without astonishment.

The following account of the length of the yards of our good old ship Impetueux, will enable a landsman, after proportionable deduction, to form some idea of the yards of a merchantman:—

	Feet.	In.
Main-yard	98	9
Top-sail-yard	69	5
Top-gallant-yard	42	2
Fore-yard	85	9
Fore-top-sail-yard	67	1
Fore-top-gallant-yard	37	2
Mizzen-top-sail-yard	47	10
Mizzen-top-gallant-yard	33	0
Cross-jack-yard	66	0
Sprit-sail-yard	64	2

P. 61, l. 324, &c. *Reef-lines, shrouds, reef-band, outer and inner turns.*

Reef-lines, are only used to reef the main-sail and fore-sail. Shrouds, so called from the Saxon Scrud, consist of a range of thick ropes stretching downwards from the mast heads, to the right and left sides of a ship, in order to support the masts, and enable them to carry sail; they are also used as rope ladders, by which seamen ascend, or descend, to execute whatever is wanting to be done about the sails and rigging. Reef-band, consists of a piece of canvas sewed across the sail, to strengthen it in the place where the eyelet-holes of the reefs are formed. The outer turns of the earing serve to extend the sail along its yard; the inner turns are employed to confine its head rope close to its surface. FALCONER.

P. 62, l. 346. *A sea, up-surging with stupendous roll.*

A sea is the general term given by sailors to an enormous wave; and hence, when such a wave bursts over the deck, the vessel is said to have shipped a sea. FALCONER.

It is impossible to peruse the dreadful effects of this event, without acknowledging the wonderful powers of our poet: I know only of one writer who has thus forcibly described the awful horrors of a watery grave: Mrs. Radcliff's Address to the Winds is worthy of Falconer; and will serve to impart kindred sensations to the reader's mind:—

"Viewless, through Heaven's vast vault your course ye steer,
Unknown from whence ye come, or whither go!
Mysterious powers! I hear ye murmur low,
Till swells your loud gust on my startled ear,
And awful, seems to say—some God is near!
I love to list your midnight voices float
In the dread storm that o'er the ocean rolls;
And while their charm the angry wave controls,
Mix with its sullen roar, and sink remote:
Then, rising in the pause, a sweeter note,
The dirge of spirits, who your deeds bewail,
A sweeter note oft swells while sleeps the gale—
But soon, ye sightless powers, your rest is o'er!
Solemn, and slow ye rise upon the air,
Speak in the shrouds, and bid the sea boy fear;
And the faint warbled dirge is heard no more.

"Oh, then I deprecate your awful reign!
The loud lament yet bear not on your breath;
Bear not the crash of bark far on the main,

Bear not the cry of men who cry in vain,
The crew's dead chorus sinking into death!
Oh give not these, ye powers! — I ask alone,
As rapt I climb these dark romantic steeps,
The elemental war! the billows moan!
I ask the still, sweet tear that list'ning fancy weeps."

P. 63, l. 376.

Too late to weather now Morea's land,
And drifting fast on Athens' rocky strand.

To weather a shore is to pass to windward of it, which at this time was prevented by the violence of the gale. Drift is that motion and direction, by which a vessel is forced to leeward sideways, when she is unable any longer to carry sail; or, at least, is restrained to such a portion of sail, as may be necessary to keep her sufficiently inclined to one side, that she may not be dismasted by her violent labouring produced by the turbulence of the sea. FALCONER.

P. 64, l. 383. *And try beneath it sidelong in the sea.*

To try, is to lay the ship with her side nearly in the direction of the wind and sea, with her head somewhat inclined to windward; the helm being fastened close to the lee side, or in the sea language, hard a-lee, to retain her in that position. See a further illustration in the last note of this canto. FALCONER.

P. 64, l. 385. *Topping-lift; knittle, throt.*

A tackle, or assemblage of pulleys, which tops the upper end of the mizzen-yard. This line, and the six following, describe the operation of reefing and balancing the mizzen. The knittle is a short line used to reef the sails by the bottom. The throt is that part of the mizzen yard, which is close to the mast.

FALCONER.

P. 64, l. 386. *The head, with doubling canvas fenced around.*

This was done to prevent any chafing of the sail when balanced. The operation of balancing is now totally disused; great improvements having been since made both in the theory and practice of seamanship. Captain Bentinck of the Royal Navy invented, and used triangular courses, which he carried with singular effect in the heaviest gales; and these courses were named after him Bentincks: since which, storm stay-sails have superseded their use; and seem to answer every purpose, either for lying-to, or giving the ship way through the water. N. P.

P. 66, l. 436.

Across the geometric plane expands
The compasses to circumjacent lands.

Here again, the third edition has been guilty of an injudicious alteration:—

"In vain athwart the mimic seas expands."

It is to be lamented that in our navy no mathematical instruments are sent on board by the admiralty. Even the master is obliged to purchase them out of his pay; and, as that is but moderate, he naturally procures the cheapest that can be obtained. One set at least of the very best that the metropolis can produce, should be sent from the board to each ship; having previously been examined by the Royal Astronomer at Greenwich. The institution of an hydrographer at the Admiralty, in order to furnish our ships with correct charts, will, probably, in time lead to the above mentioned desideratum. It is painful to observe the wretched instruments that are now in use on board; nor can the exception of a few ships, whose captains are men of independent fortunes, weaken this assertion.

P. 67, l. 458. *Companion, binacle.*

The companion is a wooden porch placed over the ladder, that leads down to the cabins of the officers. The binacle is a case, which is placed on deck before the helm, containing three divisions; the middle one for a lamp, or candle, and the two others for mariners' compasses. There are always two binacles on the deck of a ship of war, one of which is placed before the master, at his appointed station. In all the old sea books it was called bittacle. FALCONER.

P. 67, l. 464. *They sound the well.*

The well is an apartment in a ship's hold, serving to inclose the pumps: it is sounded by dropping down a measured iron rod, which is connected with a long line. The brake is the pump handle: Falconer again alludes to this iron rod, (Page 76, l. 697,) "Sounding her depth they eyed the wetted scale." A most valuable discovery was made some years since by Mr. Richard Wells, and communicated to the American Philosophical Society; by means of which vessels could be pumped at sea, without the labour of men. See also Naval Chronicle (Vol. II. p. 237.)

P. 69, l. 520. *Meanwhile Arion traversing the waist.*

The waist is that part of a ship which is contained between the quarter deck and fore-castle; or the middle of that deck which is immediately below them. When the waist of a merchant ship is only one or two steps in descent from the quarter deck and fore-castle, she is said to be galley built; but when it is considerably deeper, as with six or seven steps, she is then called frigate built. FALCONER.

P. 70, l. 540.

Cimmerian darkness shades the deep around,
Save when the lightnings in terrific blaze
Deluge the cheerless gloom with horrid rays:
Above, all ether fraught with scenes of woe.

I have already in the Life of Falconer mentioned the uncertainty that prevails, respecting the author of the favourite song, Cease, rude Boreas: in this passage additional testimony seems to arise, that it was composed by Falconer: —

"In our eyes blue lightnings flash:
One wide water all around us,
All above us one black sky!"

P. 70, l. 552. . . . . . *the booming waters roar.*

Beautifully expressive of their violence: thus Young,

" . . . . booming o'er his head
The billows closed; he's number'd with the dead!"

In the third edition, however, this epithet was expunged: —

" . . . . o'er
The sea-beat ship the involving waters roar."

P. 71, l. 577. *Her place discover'd by the rules of art.*

The lee-way, or drift, in this passage are synonymous terms. The true course and distance, resulting from these traverses, is discovered by collecting the difference of latitude, and departure of each course; and reducing the whole into one departure, and one difference of latitude, according to the known rules of trigonometry: this reduction will immediately ascertain the base and perpendicular; or, in other words, will give the difference of latitude and departure, to discover the course and distance.

FALCONER.

P. 71, l. 581. *Falconera, St. George, Gardalor.*

Falconera, a small island in the Archipelago, to the N. W. of Milo: there is an open space of sea to the North and South of it; but in every other direction are islands at no great distance. Falconer, in his chart, prefixed to the second edition, marked a line of rocks throughout the E. and S. E. coast of this island. The small and steep island of St. George is situated to the S. W. of Cape Colonna, at the entrance of the gulf of Egina. Gardalor lies off the coast of Attica, between Cape Colonna and Porto Leono.

P. 73, l. 615.

These seas, where storms at various seasons blow,
No reigning winds nor certain omens know.

It is in consequence of this that the Greeks in all ages have been excellent boatmen, and bad seamen. Mr. Mitford informs us, in the first volume of his History of Greece, that the English are the only navigators who can keep this sea in rough weather, and that they "alone, accustomed in all their surrounding waters to a bolder navigation, commonly venture in the Archipelago to work to windward." Mr. Wood, in his Essay on Homer, adds — "I remember to have heard an English captain of a Turkey ship, a man of knowledge and character, say; that he did not scruple, in tolerable weather, to work within the arches, as our seamen call the Archipelago, (which is itself a corruption of the modern Greek Aigiopelago); but he made it a rule never to take off his clothes; and, without leaving orders, to be called in the instant of any threatening appearance in the sky, or any dubious sight of land, never to quit the deck."

P. 74, l. 661.

Yet where with safety can we dare to scud
Before this tempest, and pursuing flood?

The movement of scudding, from the Swedish word skutta, is

never attempted in a contrary wind, unless, as in the present instance, the condition of a ship renders her incapable of sustaining any longer on her side, the mutual efforts of the winds and waves. The principal hazards, incident to scudding, are generally a pooping sea; the difficulty of steering, which exposes the vessel perpetually to the risk of broaching-to; and the want of sufficient sea-room: a sea striking the ship violently on the stern may dash it inwards, by which she must inevitably founder; in broaching-to suddenly, she is threatened with being immediately overset; and, for want of sea-room, she is endangered with shipwreck on a lee-shore; a circumstance too dreadful to require explanation. FALCONER.

P. 76, l. 701.

And now the senior pilots seem'd to wait
Arion's voice to close the dark debate.

The word pilots occurs too often, since it is invariably used in a sense foreign to its real meaning — the master, and mates of the vessel. The reader will here remember, under the character of Arion that of Falconer himself is described: in the speech therefore, that succeeds, we have the real sentiments of our author at this critical emergency, which, with considerable effect, he has thus reserved to close the debate.

P. 77, l. 717. *Thus water-logged* —

A ship is said to be water-logged, when, having received through her leaks a great quantity of water in her hold, she has become so heavy and inactive on the sea, as to yield without resistance to the efforts of every wave that rushes over the deck. As in this dangerous situation the centre of gravity is no longer fixed, but fluctuates from place to place, the stability of the ship is utterly lost: she is therefore almost totally deprived of the use of her sails, which operate to overset her, or press the head under water: hence there is no resource for the crew, except to free her by the pumps, or to abandon her for the boats as soon as possible. FALCONER.

P. 81, l. 830. *Hatches, lanyard.*

Falconer, to avoid repetition, has in the word hatches, employed a term which he himself in his dictionary informs us, seamen sometimes incorrectly use for gratings; a sort of open cover for the hatchways, formed by several small laths, or battens, which cross each other at right angles, leaving a square interval between: these gratings are not only of service to admit the air and light between decks, but also to let off the smoke of the great guns during action.

Lanyard, or laniard, is a short piece of line fastened to different things on board a ship, to preserve them in a particular place; such are the lanyards of the gun ports, the lanyard of the buoy, the lanyard of the cat hook, &c. but the lanyards alluded to in the above line, were those, by means of which the shrouds were kept extended; or, as a sailor would express himself, taught.

P. 84, l. 901. *Both stay-sail sheets to mid-ships were convey'd.*

The fore stay-sail being one of the sails which command the fore part of the ship, is for that reason hoisted at this time, to bear her fore part round before the wind: for the same reason, after it is split, the foremost yards are braced aback; that is, so as to form right angles with the direction of the wind. For a further illustration of this, see the subsequent note.

FALCONER.

P. 84, l. 914. *And hew at once the mizzen-mast away!*

In addition to the nautical notes by Falconer, the following illustration of the orders that have been given by Albert, was subjoined by our author to the second edition. — "When a ship is forced by the violence of a contrary wind to furl all her sails, if the storm increases, and the sea continue to rise, she is often strained to so great a degree, that, to ease her, she must be made to run before their mutual direction; which however is rarely done but in cases of the last necessity: now as she has no head-way the helm is deprived of its governing power, as the latter effect is only produced in consequence of the former: it therefore necessarily requires an uncommon effort to wheel, or turn her, into any different position. It is an axiom in natural philosophy, that, 'Every body will persevere in its state of rest, or moving uniformly in a right line, unless it be compelled to change its state by forces impressed; and that the change of motion is proportional to the moving force impressed, and is made according to the right line in which that force acts.'

"By this principle it is easy to conceive, how a ship is compelled to turn into any direction, by the force of the wind acting upon her sails in lines parallel to the plane of the horizon; for the sails may be so set, as to receive the current of air either directly, or more or less obliquely; and the motion communicated to the ship must of necessity conspire with that of the wind. As therefore the ship lies in such a situation as to have the wind and sea directly on her side; and these increase to such a height, that she must either founder, or scud before the storm; the aftmost sails are first taken in, or so placed that the wind has very little power on them; and the head-sails, or foremost sails, are spread abroad, so that the whole force of the wind is exerted on the ship's fore-part, which must therefore of necessity yield to its impulse. The prow being thus put in motion, its motion must conspire with that of the wind, and will be pushed about so as to run immediately before it: for this reason, when no more sail can be carried, the foremost yards are braced aback, that is, in such a position as to receive all the current of air they can contain directly to perform the operation of head-sails; and the mizzen-yard is lowered to produce the same effect as furling, or placing obliquely the aftmost sails; and this attempt being found insufficient, the mizzen-mast is cut away, which must have been followed by the main-mast, if the expected effect had not taken place."

CANTO III.

P. 89, l. 1. *When in a barbarous age, &c.*

These beautiful introductory reflections on the beneficial influence of poetry, as promoting the civilization, and consequently the happiness of mankind, form an unanswerable reply to the enthusiastic ravings of Rousseau, and his fellow madmen; who have attempted to raise the character of the human savage, above the mind that has been polished with the embellishments of social life.

P. 91, l. 65.

While round before the enlarging wind it falls,
"Square fore and aft the yards," the master calls.

The wind is said to enlarge, when it veers from the side towards the stern. To square the yards is, in this place, to haul them directly across the ship's length. FALCONER.

P. 92, l. 69. *So, steady! meet her!*

Steady! is an order to steer the ship according to the line on which she then advances, without deviating to the right, or left.
FALCONER.

P. 92, l. 73. *Then back to port, &c.*

The left side of a ship is called port in steering, that the helmsmen may not mistake larboard for starboard. In all large ships, the tiller, (or long bar of timber, that is fixed horizontally to the upper end of the rudder,) is guided by a wheel, which acts upon it with the powers of a crane, or windlass. FALCONER.

P. 93, l. 99. *As that rebellious angel, &c.*

This allusion to the flight of Satan from hell, forms one of the most beautiful similes in the poem. It is described by Milton in two separate passages at the conclusion of his second book of Paradise Lost.

P. 93, l. 113. *Poop, bow.*

Poop, from the Latin word puppis, is the hindmost, and highest deck of a ship. The bow is the rounding part of a ship's side forward, beginning at the place where the planks arch inwards, and terminating where they close at the stem, or prow.

FALCONER.

P. 94, l. 129. . . . . *when past the beam it flies.*

On the beam, implies any distance from the ship on a line with the beams, or at right angles with the keel: thus, if the ship steers northward, any object lying east of west, is said to be on her starboard, or larboard beam. FALCONER.

P. 95, l. 154.

They did: for in this desert, joyless soil,
No flowers of genial science deign to smile.

The whole of what follows would have been more clearly expressed, had our author substituted our, for this: since the reader is at first troubled to find out, whether the soil of the classic territory of Greece is not alluded to—

"They did: for in our desert, joyless soil—"

Or in our uneducated miserable profession, no love of science, or of literature, ever appears.

In these and the following lines, Falconer very unjustly abuses the taste, and classical acquirements of naval officers: his own mind was alone sufficient to contradict such an assertion. No profession whatever cherishes with more assiduity the "flowers of genial science," and the glowing numbers of poesy, than the British Navy. To the name of Falconer may be added that of Mickle, and many others, who were, as Mr. Pye says,

"Nursed on the waves, and cradled in the storm."

Nor can I allow, that ocean's genius withers the bloom of every springing flower: the sublime Camoens composed the greater part of his Lusiadas at sea, under the immediate influence of this genius; and, if I were requested to select a person, whose taste for poetry, and other classic acquirements, was superior to that of the rest of mankind, I should be justified in mentioning a name, which will ever be engraven on my heart — the late Admiral J. W. Payne.

P. 96, l. 178.

Immortal Athens first, in ruin spread,
Contiguous lies at Port Liono's head.

Porto Leone, the ancient Piræum, received its modern title from a large lion of white marble, since carried by the Venetians to their arsenal. The ports of ancient Athens were — 1. Phalerim; 2. Munichia; and 3. Pyræus, the most capacious.

A particular account of modern Athens, or as it is now called Athini, is given by Dr. Chandler: it was also visited by Lord Sandwich in his voyage round the Mediterranean. Its antiquities have been amply described by Le Roy, and Stuart. I have already mentioned the dangerous navigation of the Archipelago, and it is considerably increased as you advance towards Porto Leone; particularly if the ship is of any great burden. At the close of the year 1802, the Braakel of 54 guns, commanded by my brother Capt. George Clarke, was sent on this hazardous service; which he accomplished at the most imminent risk — the following extract from his letter will illustrate the danger which Falconer so well describes: "From the ignorance of the pilot, the Braakel, when in stays, struck at midnight on a point of land, that forms the entrance of the harbour of Porto Leone, eight miles from the town of Athens. I contrived to land a quantity of provisions on the rocks, and was obliged to order half the guns to be hove overboard; at the same time a sheet anchor, and cable, were got out astern to heave the ship off, which we in vain attempted for many hours: at length, to our great joy, being assisted by the wind coming strong right off the land, we swung round off, and rode stern to wind by the above mentioned anchor. In about an hour the weather changed; the wind shifted, and placed the ship with a strong gale, and heavy sea, close to the shore. The cable was instantly cut, and we made sail to get round the northern extremity of the point; when the pilot again mistaking the land, we anchored in a wrong position, yet clear of the rocks; until the wind shifting, placed the ship in the middle of a second dark stormy night. We came slap on shore, along-side the rocks; fortunately the ship lay tolerably easy, being assisted by the anchor; which owing to the wind shifting, brought it well out on the starboard bow. Day-break at length appeared, and the gale shifted again: hove on the anchor, and succeeded in getting her off after a few hard knocks, the loss of a little copper, and part of the false keel. Made sail again, weathered our danger, and anchored for want of wind; when a breeze springing up, we got safe into Porto Leone. In performing this we lost the sheet anchor, the stream, and the kedge. On leaving this harbour we were driven back three times: when I bore up for Port Oliver, in the island of Metelin, where there is a harbour beyond description safe, and spacious. I do not think this is generally known; or what is more, that the Turks build frigates there; one of 32 guns was at this time on the stocks."

G. C.

P. 98, l. 243. *That pipes among The Shades of Endermay.*

A song entitled the Birks of Endermay was written by Mallet, and is mentioned by Dr. Currie in his Life of Burns. (Page 278.)

P. 100, l. 287. *No human footstep marks the trackless sand.*

And thus Petrarch,

Dove vestigio uman l'arena stampi. F. D.

P. 101, l. 311. *The seat of sacred Troy is found no more.*

Amidst the disputes that have harassed the learned world on this subject, I am glad to subjoin the opinion of my brother, fellow of Jesus College, Cambridge, who has so lately visited Troy; and, after a minute examination of every particular on the spot, has been convinced that such a city did exist, as was described by Homer. — " Travellers visiting the plain of Troy in search of columns, or statues, by which the site of ancient Ilium may be determined, are not less idly occupied, than those persons who have pretended to discover such remains: the latter class have fallen into the error of the painter, employed by Comte de Caylus, (see Winkelman, liv. iv. ch. 8, note,) to illustrate the picture by Polygnotus at Delphi, according to Pausanius; who ornamented the city of Troy with columns and statues of marble — monuments of the arts, that were unknown at the time of the Trojan war. All that we can expect to discover, in order to identify the scene of that war, are the features of nature as described by Homer; and these are found, precisely answering his description." E. D. C. Dr. Chandler has lately considered this subject in his History of Troy.

P, 101, l. 320.

Whose gleam directed loved Leander o'er
The rolling Hellespont ——

A few years since, a servant of the Neapolitan Consul at the Dardanelles, swam across the Hellespont; and, after a short walk on the Asiatic coast, returned back in safety, notwithstanding the extreme rapidity of the current. E. D. C.

P. 102, l. 333. *Remote from ocean lies the Delphic plain.*

Falconer very properly writes Delphic. Swift made a point of writing Delphos, instead of Delphi; and until I had perused Bentley's Dissertation on Phalaris, I thought it should be thus written. Jortin, on this account, says of Swift, that "he should have received instruction from whatever quarter it came; from Wotton, from Bentley, or from Beelzebub." —It was my relation, Dr. Wotton, who first noticed the absurd use of Delphos for Delphi: see the above Dissertation, (Preface, page 46,) where Bentley defends Dr. Wotton's opinion.

Few travellers have visited Delphi, although it is perhaps the most interesting, even in its present state, of all that were Grecian cities. Some remains of its celebrated temples may still be seen, astonishing by their prodigious size and workmanship. But the beauty of the Castalian spring, adorned with wild and hanging foliage, surrounded by the precipices, and rocks of Parnassus, is unequalled. E. D. C.

P. 105, l. 409. *The impelling floods, that lash her to the shore.*

Falconer was too fond of similes, particularly in the third edition, where the following was introduced after the above line: —

"As some benighted traveller, through the shade,
Explores the devious path with heart dismay'd;
While prowling savages behind him roar,
And yawning pits, and quagmires lurk before —"

And after line 409 in the same page,

"As some fell conqueror, frantic with success,
Sheds o'er the nations ruin and distress."

Both these similes come too quick after that of the retreating army. In this, and other similar instances, I have preferred the second edition.

P. 105.

After line 425 the second edition reads,

"Such flaming horror Amos' * son foretold,
Down-rushing on the Assyrian king of old."

And in the same page, subsequent to the fourth line, in the same edition,

"Aghast on deck the shivering wretches stood,
While fear and chill despair congeal'd their blood:
And lo! all terrible, the King of kings
Through the sad sky, array'd in lightning, springs:
Tremendous panoply! his right arm bare
Red burning, shoots destruction through the air!
Hark! his strong voice," &c.

After the two lines that follow, are also inserted,

"Wide bursts in dazzling sheets the sulphur'd flame,
And dread concussion rends the ethereal frame:
Not fiercer tremors shook the world beneath,
When, writhing in the pangs of cruel death,
The sacred Lord of life resign'd his breath."

P. 106, l. 453. *Forth issues o'er the wave the weeping morn!*

It is to be lamented that Falconer did not here describe that beautiful phenomenon called the marine rainbow, which is sometimes observed in a sea much agitated. Twenty or thirty may be seen together, and in a position opposite to that of the common bow. The Weeping Morn has been selected by Mr. Pocock as the subject of a large marine picture, which he executed with his usual genius.

---

* Isaiah, chap. xxx.

P. 108, l. 489. *Still they dread her broaching-to.*

The great difficulty of steering the ship at this time before the wind, is occasioned by its striking her on the quarter, when she makes the least angle on either side; which often forces her stern round, and brings her broadside to the wind and sea: this is an effect of the same cause which is explained in the last note of the second canto. FALCONER.

P. 108, l. 496.

Not half so dreadful to Æneas' eyes
The straits of Sicily were seen to rise.

Alluding to the following beautiful passage in Virgil, (Æneid. III. v. 554):

"Tum procul è fluctu Trinacria cernitur Ætna,
Et gemitum ingentem Pelagi, pulsataque saxa
Audimus longè, fractasque ad littora voces;
Exultantque vada, atque æstu miscenter arenæ.
Et pater Anchises: 'Nimirùm hæc illa Charybdis:
Hos Helenus scopulos, hæc saxa horrenda canebat.
Eripite, ô Socii, paritérque insurgite remis.'
Haud minùs, ac jussi, faciunt: primusque rudentem
Contorsit lævas proram Palinurus ad undas:
Lævam cuncta cohors remis, ventisque petivit.
Tollimur in cœlum curvato gurgite, et iidem
Subductâ ad manes imos descendimus undâ.
Ter scopuli clamorem inter cava saxa dedêre;
Ter spuman elisam, et rorantia vidimus astra."

After this allusion, the second edition inserts the following lines:—

"So they attempt St. George's shoals to clear,
Which close beneath the larboard beam appear."

P. 110, l. 560.

The vessel, while the dread event draws nigh,
Seems more impatient o'er the waves to fly.

An idea equally correct and beautiful, and well understood by all who have been engaged with a lee shore. Having occasion to wear, the mind anxious, and care-worn, becomes impatient to try the other tack; and therefore fancies that the vessel flies towards danger, with unwonted celerity. N. P.

P. 111, l. 582. . . . . . . *the faithful stay*
Drags the main top-mast by the cap away.

The main top-mast stay comes to the fore-mast head, and consequently depends upon the fore-mast as its support. The cap is a strong, thick block of wood, used to confine the upper and lower masts together, as the one is raised at the head of the other. The principal caps of a ship are those of the lower masts.
FALCONER.

P. 113, l. 632. *For every wave now smites the quivering yard.*

The sea at this time ran so high, that it was impossible to descend from the mast-head without being washed overboard.
FALCONER.

P. 119, l. 793, &c.

Down from his neck, with blazing gems array'd,
Thy image, lovely Anna! hung portray'd;
The unconscious figure, smiling all serene.

This image of the calm, unconscious portrait, is a most poetical, new, and striking combination. W. L. B.

P. 123, l. 873. *Oh! then, to swell the tides of social woe.*

After this line, the second edition reads,

"Thou, who hast taught the tragic harp to mourn
In early youth o'er Frederic's royal urn."

P. 123, l. 882. *All thoughts of happiness on earth are vain!*

" . . . . sed scilicet ultima semper
Expectanda dies homini; dicique beatus
Ante obitum nemo supremaque funera debet."

FALCONER.

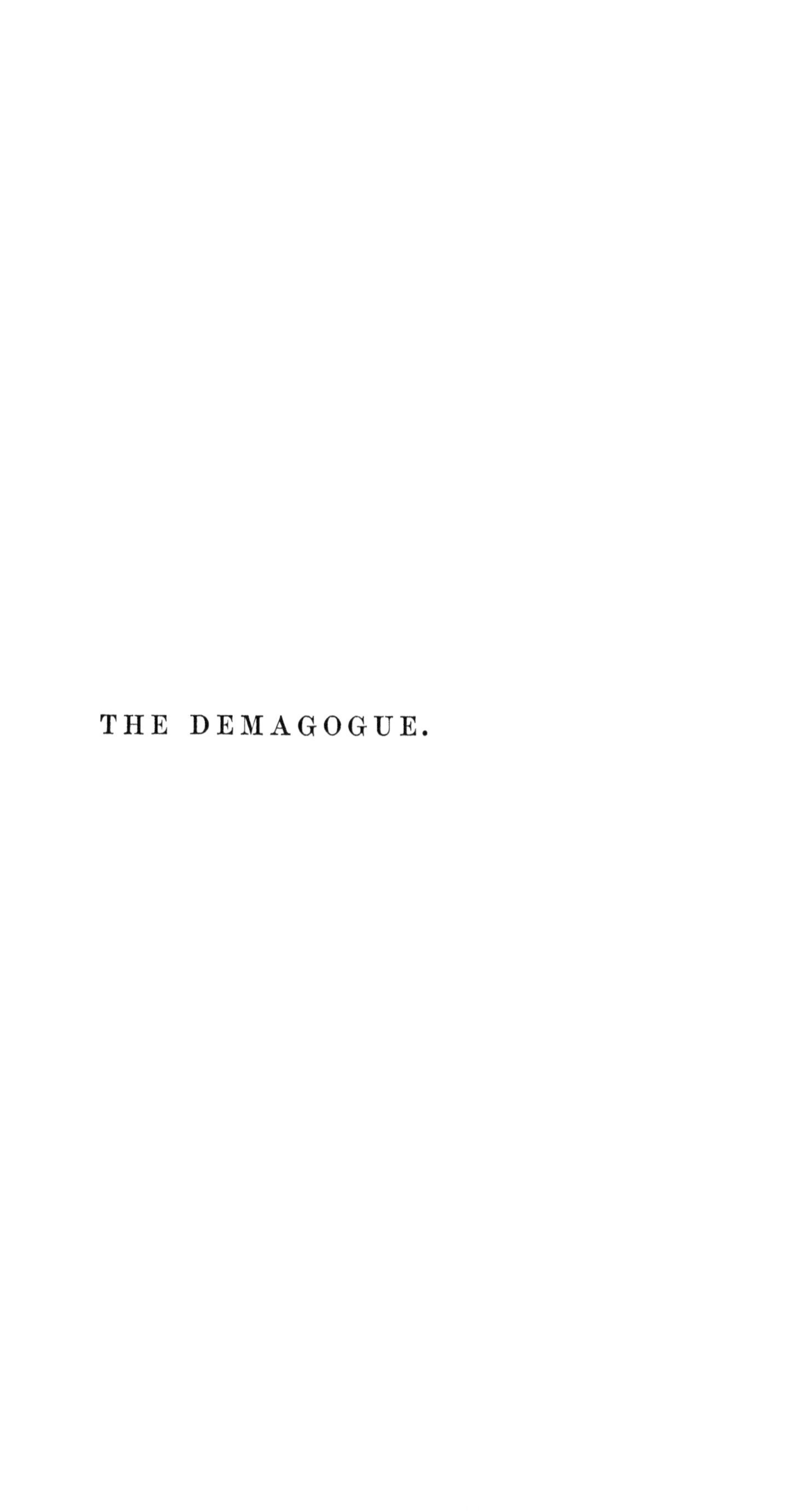

THE DEMAGOGUE.

THE DEMAGOGUE.

Bold is the attempt, in these licentious times,
When with such towering strides sedition climbs,
With sense or satire to confront her power,
And charge her in the great decisive hour:
Bold is the man, who, on her conquering day,
Stands in the pass of fate to bar her way:
Whose heart, by frowning arrogance unawed,
Or the deep-lurking snares of specious fraud,
The threats of giant-faction can deride,
And stem, with stubborn arm, her roaring tide.
For him unnumber'd brooding ills await,
Scorn, malice, insolence, reproach, and hate:
At him, who dares this legion to defy,
A thousand mortal shafts in secret fly:
Revenge, exulting with malignant joy,
Pursues the incautious victim to destroy:
And slander strives, with unrelenting aim,
To spit her blasting venom on his name:
Around him faction's harpies flap their wings,
And rhyming vermin dart their feeble stings:

In vain the wretch retreats, while in full cry,
Fierce on his throat the hungry bloodhounds fly.
Enclosed with perils thus the conscious muse,
Alarm'd, though undismay'd, her danger views.
Nor shall unmanly terror now control
The strong resentment struggling in her soul;
While indignation, with resistless strain,
Pours her full deluge through each swelling vein.
By the vile fear that chills the coward breast,
By sordid caution is her voice supprest,
While arrogance, with big theatric rage,
Audacious struts on power's imperial stage;
While o'er our country, at her dread command,
Black discord, screaming, shakes her fatal brand:
While, in defiance of maternal laws,
The sacrilegious sword rebellion draws;
Shall she at this important hour retire,
And quench in Lethe's wave her genuine fire?
Honour forbid! she fears no threat'ning foe,
When conscious justice bids her bosom glow:
And while she kindles the reluctant flame,
Let not the prudent voice of friendship blame!
She feels the sting of keen resentment goad,
Though guiltless yet of satire's thorny road.
Let other Quixotes, frantic with renown,
Plant on their brows a tawdry paper crown!

While fools adore, and vassal-bards obey,
Let the great monarch ass through Gotham bray!
Our poet brandishes no mimic sword,
To rule a realm of dunces self-explored:
No bleeding victims curse his iron sway;
Nor murder'd reputation marks his way.
True to herself, unarm'd, the fearless muse
Thro' reason's path her steady course pursues:
True to herself advances, undeterr'd
By the rude clamours of the savage herd.
As some bold surgeon, with inserted steel,
Probes deep the putrid sore, intent to heal;
So the rank ulcers that our patriot load,
Shall she with caustic's healing fires corrode.
Yet ere from patient slumber satire wakes,
And brandishes the avenging scourge of snakes;
Yet ere her eyes, with lightning's vivid ray,
The dark recesses of his heart display;
Let candour own the undaunted pilot's power,
Felt in severest danger's trying hour!
Let truth consenting, with the trump of fame!
His glory, in auspicious strains, proclaim!
He bade the tempest of the battle roar,
That thunder'd o'er the deep from shore to shore.
How oft, amid the horrors of the war,
Chain'd to the bloody wheels of danger's car,

How oft my bosom at thy name has glow'd,
And from my beating heart applause bestow'd;
Applause, that, genuine as the blush of youth
Unknown to guile, was sanctified by truth!
How oft I blest the patriot's honest rage,
That greatly dared to lash the guilty age;
That, rapt with zeal, pathetic, bold, and strong,
Roll'd the full tide of eloquence along;
That power's big torrent braved with manly pride,
And all corruption's venal arts defied!
When from afar those penetrating eyes
Beheld each secret hostile scheme arise;
Watch'd every motion of the faithless foe,
Each plot o'erturn'd, and baffled every blow:
A fond enthusiast, kindling at thy name,
I glow'd in secret with congenial flame;
While my young bosom, to deceit unknown,
Believed all real virtue thine alone.

Such then he seem'd, and such indeed might be,
If truth with error ever could agree!
Sure satire never with a fairer hand
Portray'd the object she design'd to brand.
Alas! that virtue should so soon decay,
And faction's wild applause thy heart betray!
The muse with secret sympathy relents,
And human failings, as a friend, laments:

But when those dangerous errors, big with fate,
Spread discord and distraction through the state,
Reason should then exert her utmost power
To guard our passions in that fatal hour.
There was a time, ere yet his conscious heart
Durst from the hardy path of truth depart,
While yet with generous sentiment it glow'd,
A stranger to corruption's slippery road;
There was a time our patriot durst avow
Those honest maxims he despises now.
How did he then his country's wounds bewail,
And at the insatiate German vulture rail!
Whose cruel talons Albion's entrails tore,
Whose hungry maw was glutted with her gore?
The mists of error, that in darkness held
Our reason, like the sun, his voice dispell'd.
And lo! exhausted, with no power to save,
We view Britannia panting on the wave;
Hung round her neck, a millstone's pond'rous weight
Drags down the struggling victim to her fate!
While horror at the thought our bosom feels,
We bless the man this horror who reveals.
But what alarming thoughts the heart amaze,
When on this Janus' other face we gaze;
For, lo! possest of power's imperial reins,
Our chief those visionary ills disdains!

Alas! how soon the steady patriot turns!
In vain this change astonish'd England mourns!
Her vital blood, that pour'd from every vein,
So late, to fill the accursed Westphalian drain,
Then ceased to flow; the vulture now no more
With unrelenting rage her bowels tore.
His magic rod transforms the bird of prey!
The millstone feels the touch and melts away!
And, strange to tell, still stranger to believe,
What eyes ne'er saw, and heart could ne'er conceive,
At once, transplanted by the sorcerer's wand,
Columbian hills in distant Austria stand!
America, with pangs before unknown,
Now with Westphalia utters groan for groan:
By sympathy she fevers with her fires,
Burns as she burns, and as she dies expires.
From maxims long adopted thus he flew,
For ever changing, yet for ever true;
Swoln with success, and with applause inflamed,
He scorn'd all caution, all advice disclaim'd;
Arm'd with war's thunder, he embraced no more
Those patriot principles maintain'd before.
Perverse, inconstant, obstinate, and proud,
Drunk with ambition, turbulent and loud,
He wrecks us headlong on that dreadful strand
He once devoted all his powers to brand!

Our hapless country views with weeping eyes,
On every side, o'erwhelming horrors rise;
Drain'd of her wealth, exhausted of her power,
And agonized as in the mortal hour;
Her armies wasted with incessant toils,
Or doom'd to perish in contagious soils,
To guard some needy royal plunderer's throne,
And sent to fall in battles not their own.
The enormous debt at home, tho' long o'ercharged,
With grievous burdens annually enlarged:
Crush'd with increasing taxes to the ground,
That suck, like vampires, every bleeding wound:
Ground with severe distress the industrious poor,
Driven by the ruthless landlord to the door.
While thus our land her hapless fate bemoans
In secret, and with inward sorrow groans;
Though deck'd with tinsel trophies of renown,
All gash'd with sores, with anguish bending down,
Can yet some impious parricide appear,
Who strives to make this anguish more severe?
Can one exist, so much his country's foe,
To bid her wounds with fresh effusion flow?
There can; to him in vain she lifts her eyes,
His soul relentless hears her piercing sighs!
Shameless of front, impatient of control,
He spurs her onward to destruction's goal!

Nor yet content on curst Westphalia's shore
With mad profusion to exhaust her store,
Still peace his pompous fulminations brand,
As pirates tremble at the sight of land:
Still to new wars the public eye he turns,
Defies all peril, and at reason spurns;
Till prest with danger, by distress assail'd,
That baffled courage, and o'er skill prevail'd;
Till foundering in the storm himself had brew'd,
He strives at last its horrors to elude.
Some wretched shift must still protect his name,
And to the guiltless head transfer his shame:
Then hearing modest diffidence oppose
His rash advice, that golden time he chose;
And while big surges threaten'd to o'erwhelm
The ship, ingloriously forsook the helm.

But all the events collected to relate,
Let us his actions recapitulate.

He first assum'd, by mean perfidious art,
Those patriot tenets foreign to his heart:
Next, by his country's fond applauses swell'd,
Thrust himself forward into power, and held
The reins on principles which he alone,
Grown drunk and wanton with success, could own;
Betray'd her interest and abused her trust;
Then, deaf to prayers, forsook her in disgust;

With tragic mummery, and most vile grimace,
Rode through the city with a woful face,
As in distress, a patriot out of place!
Insults his generous prince, and in the day
Of trouble skulks, because he cannot sway!
In foreign climes embroils him with allies!
And bids at home the flames of discord rise!
She comes! from hell the exulting fury springs!
With grim destruction sailing on her wings!
Around her scream a hundred harpies fell!
A hundred demons shriek with hideous yell!
From where, in mortal venom dipt on high,
Full-drawn the deadliest shafts of satire fly,
Where Churchill brandishes his clumsy club,
And Wilkes unloads his excremental tub,
Down to where Entick, awkward and unclean,
Crawls on his native dust, a worm obscene!
While with unnumber'd wings, from van to rear,
Myriads of nameless buzzing drones appear:
From their dark cells the angry insects swarm,
And every little sting attempt to arm.
Here Chaplains,* Privileges,* moulder round,
And feeble Scourges,* rot upon the ground:

* Certain poems intended to be very satirical; but, alas! we refer our reader to the Reviews.

Here hungry Kenrick strives, with fruitless aim,
With Grub-street slander to extend his name:
At Bruin flies the slavering, snarling cur,
But only fills his famish'd jaws with fur.
Here Baldwin spreads the assassinating cloke,
Where lurking rancour gives the secret stroke;
While gorg'd with filth, around this senseless block,
A swarm of spider-bards obsequious flock:
While his demure Welch goat, with lifted hoof,
In Poet's-corner hangs each flimsy woof:
And frisky grown, attempts, with awkward prance,
On wit's gay theatre to bleat and dance.
Here, seiz'd with iliac passion, mouthing Leech,
Too low, alas! for satire's whip to reach,
From his black entrails, faction's common sewer,
Disgorges all her excremental store.

With equal pity and regret the muse
The thundering storms that rage around her views;
Impartial views the tides of discord blend,
Where lordly rogues for power and place contend;
Were not her patriot heart with anguish torn,
Would eye the opposing chiefs with equal scorn.
Let freedom's deadliest foes for freedom bawl,
Alike to her who govern or who fall!
Aloof she stands, all unconcern'd and mute,
While the rude rabble bellow, "Down with Bute!"

While villany the scourge of justice bilks,
Howl on, ye ruffians! "Liberty and Wilkes."
Let some soft mummy of a peer, who stains
His rank, some sodden lump of ass's brains,
To that abandon'd wretch his sanction give;
Support his slander, and his wants relieve!
Let the great hydra roar aloud for Pitt,
And power and wisdom all to him submit!
Let proud ambition's sons, with hearts severe,
Like parricides, their mother's bowels tear!
Sedition her triumphant flag display,
And in embodied ranks her troops array!
While coward justice, trembling on her seat,
Like a vile slave descends to lick her feet!
Nor here let censure draw her awful blade,
If from her theme the wayward muse has stray'd!
Sometimes the impetuous torrent, o'er its mounds
Redundant bursting, swamps the adjacent grounds;
But rapid, and impatient of delay,
Through the deep channel still pursues its way.
Our pilot now retired, no pleasure knows,
But every man and measure to oppose;
Like Æsop's cur, still snarling and perverse,
Bloated with envy, to mankind a curse,
No more at council his advice will lend,
But with all others who advise contend:

He bids distraction o'er his country blaze,
Then, swelter'd with revenge, retreats to Hayes: *

* After reflecting on the various events by which this extraordinary person is characterized, we cannot resist the temptation of quoting a few anecdotes from Machiavel, relative to a man of a very similar complexion and constitution, who was also distinguished by a train of incidents pretty nearly resembling those we have mentioned above; although he possibly never anticipated the similitude of fortune and character that might happen between him and any of his progeny. Speaking of the government of Florence, our historian informs us, that "Luca Pitt, a bold and resolute man, being now made gonsalionere of justice, having entered upon his office, was very importunate with the people to appoint a balia; but perceiving it was to no purpose, he not only treated those that were members of the council with great insolence, and called them opprobrious names, but threatened them, and soon after put his threats in execution: for having filled the palace with armed men, on the eve of St. Lorenzo, in the month of August, 1453, he called the people together into the piazza, and there compelled them, by force of arms, to do that which they would not so much as hear of before. Pitt had also very rich presents, not only from Cosimo and the signiory, but from all the principal citizens, who vied with each other in their generosity to him; so that it was thought he had above twenty thousand ducats given him at that time; after which he became so popular, that the city was no longer governed by Cosimo di Medici, but by Luca Pitt. This inspired him with vanity. After this he had recourse to very extraordinary means; for he not only extorted more and greater presents from the chief citizens, but also made the commonalty supply him with workmen and artificers," Machiavel's Hist. Florence. This has an unlucky resemblance to a certain great person's driving through the city with borrowed horses, and being offered to have his horses unyoked, and his chariot drawn by his good friends the mob. We shall, in due time and place, give some account of the fall of Mr. Luca Pitt, and the contempt with which, after some particular events, he was universally regarded.

Swallows the pension; but, aware of blame,
Transfers the proffer'd peerage to his dame.
The felon thus of old, his name to save,
His pilfer'd mutton to a brother gave.
But should some frantic wretch, whom all men know
To nature and humanity a foe,
Deaf to the widow's moan and orphan's cry,
And dead to shame and friendship's social tie;
Should such a miscreant, at the hour of death,
To thee his fortunes and domains bequeath;
With cruel rancour wresting from his heirs
What nature taught them to expect as theirs;
Wouldst thou with this detested robber join,
Their legal wealth to plunder and purloin?
Forbid it, Heaven! thou canst not be so base,
To blast thy name with infamous disgrace!
The muse who wakes, yet triumphs o'er thy hate,
Dares not so black a thought anticipate:
By Heaven, the muse her ignorance betrays;
For while a thousand eyes with wonder gaze,
Tho' gorged and glutted with his country's store,
The vulture pounces on the shining ore;
In his strong talons gripes the golden prey,
And from the weeping orphan bears away.
The great, the alarming deed is yet to come,

That, big with fate, strikes expectation dumb.
O! patient, injured England, yet unveil
Thy eyes, and listen to the muse's tale,
That true as honour, unadorn'd with art,
Thy wrongs in fair succession shall impart!
  Ere yet the desolating god of war
Had crush'd pale Europe with his iron car,
Had shook her shores with terrible alarms,
And thunder'd o'er the trembling deep, "To arms!"
In climes remote, beyond the setting sun,
Beyond the Atlantic wave, his rage begun.
Alas! poor country, how with pangs unknown
To Britain did thy filial bosom groan!
What savage armies did thy realms invade,
Unarm'd, and distant from maternal aid!
Thy cottages with cruel flames consumed,
And the sad owner to destruction doom'd;
Mangled with wounds, with pungent anguish torn,
Or left to perish naked and forlorn!
What carnage reek'd upon thy ruin'd plain!
What infants bled! what virgins shriek'd in vain!
In every look distraction seem'd to glare,
Each heart was rack'd with horror and despair.
To Albion then, with groans and piercing cries,
America lift up her dying eyes;
To generous Albion pour'd forth all her pain,

To whom the wretched never wept in vain.
She heard, and instant to relieve her flew,
Her arm the gleaming sword of vengeance drew;
Far o'er the ocean wave her voice was known,
That shook the deep abyss from zone to zone:
She bade the thunder of the battle glow,
And pour'd the storm of lightning on the foe;
Nor ceased till, crown'd with victory complete,
Pale Spain and France lay trembling at her feet.*

---

* Although our author has no present inclination to enter into political controversy, yet he cannot avoid citing an article from one of the modern dictionaries, which in some measure is connected with this part of his subject, and exhibits a view of the fidelity and gratitude of our fellow-subjects in America.

We are informed in the article referred to, that a "cartel in the marine is a ship provided in time of war to exchange the prisoners of any two hostile powers; also to carry any particular request or proposal from the one to the other: for this reason she is particularly commanded to carry no cargo or arms, only a single gun for firing signals.

"Our honest Americans, however, who have so sorely grieved of late for paying a small part of the great taxes of this country, although demanded for their own particular protection, made not only no scruple to disobey and despise this regulation of cartels during the late war, but, on the contrary, gave continual supplies of provisions to our enemies in the West Indies, and thereby recovered them, and recruited their fallen spirits, at a time when they were gasping under the weight of our arms. With so much address, indeed, did these oppressed and unfortunate traders conduct this scheme, that ten or twelve cartels being laden at the same time with beef, pork, bread, flour, &c. sailed together for the French islands, and, in order to evade the strict examination of our ships of war, were provided with a

Her fears dispell'd, and all her foes removed,
Her fertile grounds industriously improved,

---

guardian privateer, equipped by the same expert owners, to seize their own vessels, and direct their course to the places of their first destination; but if they were examined by our ships of war, to an English port. But this clumsy trick did not long escape the vigilance of our naval officers, who found that the fellows sent abroad, by way of commanders or prize-masters, were utterly ignorant, and incapable of piloting any ship; and of consequence only sent to elude their scrutiny.

"The most barefaced piece of effrontery, however, that was ever committed of this kind, was the seizing an armed vessel, fitted in Philadelphia, to take these illegal cartels. She was commanded by a gentleman, whom the majority of the merchants in that city joined to oppose and distress. They employed a crew of ruffians, who seized his vessel openly, in the most unwarranted and lawless manner, and brought her up in triumph to the town, when she had only five men aboard: and so inveterate was their hatred to the commander, that he was obliged to leave the country precipitately, as being in danger of his life."

There cannot be a stronger confirmation of the truth of the above account, than the following letter of Mr. Pitt: —

Copy of a letter from Mr. Secretary Pitt to the several governors and councils in North America, relating to the flag of truce trade.

"Whitehall, August 24, 1760.

"Gentlemen,

"The commanders of his majesty's forces and fleets in North America and the West Indies have transmitted certain and repeated intelligences of an illegal and most pernicious trade carried on by the king's subjects in North America and the West Indies, as well to the French islands as to the French settlements on the continent in America, and particularly to the rivers Mobile and Mississippi; by which the enemies, to the great reproach and detriment of government, are supplied with

Her towns with trade, with fleets her harbours
crown'd,
And plenty smiling on her plains around;
Thus blest with all that commerce could supply,
America regards with jealous eye,

---

provisions and other necessaries; whereby they are principally, if not alone, enabled to sustain and protract this long and expensive war. And it further appearing, that large sums of bullion are sent by the king's subjects to the above places, in return whereof commodities are taken, which interfere with the product of the British colonies themselves, in open contempt of the authority of the mother-country, as well as the most manifest prejudice of the manufacturers and trade of Great Britain: in order, therefore, to put the most speedy and effectual stop to such flagitious practices, so utterly subversive of all laws, and so highly repugnant to the well-being of this kingdom:

"It is his majesty's express will and pleasure, that you do forthwith make the strictest and most diligent inquiry into the state of this dangerous and ignominious trade; and that you do use every means in your power to detect and discover persons concerned either as principals or accessaries therein; and that you do take every step authorized by law to bring all such heinous offenders to the most exemplary and condign punishment: and you will, as soon as may be, and from time to time transmit to me, for the king's information, full and particular accounts of the progress you shall have made in the execution of this his majesty's commands, to the which the king expects that you pay the most exact obedience. And you are further to use your utmost endeavours to trace out and investigate the various artifices and evasions by which the dealers in this iniquitous intercourse find means to cover their criminal proceedings, and to elude the law; in order that from such lights due and timely considerations may be had what further provision may be necessary to restrain an evil of such extensive and pernicious consequences. I am, &c."

And canker'd heart, the parent, who so late
Had snatch'd her gasping from the jaws of fate;
Who now, with wars for her begun, relax'd,
With grievous aggravated burdens tax'd,
Her treasures wasted by a hungry brood
Of cormorants, that suck her vital blood;
Who now of her demands that tribute due,
For whom alone the avenging sword she drew.
  Scarce had America the just request
Received, when kindling in her faithless breast
Resentment glows, enraged sedition burns,
And, lo! the mandate of our laws she spurns!
Her secret hate, incapable of shame
Or gratitude, incenses to a flame,
Derides our power, bids insurrection rise,
Insults our honour, and our laws defies;
O'er all her coasts is heard the audacious roar,
"England shall rule America no more!"
  Soon as on Britain's shore the alarm was heard,
Stern indignation in her look appear'd;
Yet, loth to punish, she her scourge withheld
From her perfidious sons who thus rebell'd:
Now stung with anguish, now with rage assail'd,
Till pity in her soul at last prevail'd,
Determined not to draw her penal steel
Till fair persuasion made her last appeal.

And now the great decisive hour drew nigh,
She on her darling patriot cast her eye;
His voice like thunder will support her cause,
Enforce her dictates, and sustain her laws;
Rich with her spoils, his sanction will dismay,
And bid the insurgents tremble and obey.
He comes! — but where, the amazing theme to hit,
Discover language or ideas fit?
Splay-footed words, that hector, bounce, and swagger,
The sense to puzzle, and the brain to stagger?
Our patriot comes! with frenzy fired, the muse
With allegoric eye his figure views!
Like the grim portress of hell-gate he stands,
Bellona's scourge hangs trembling in his hands!
Around him, fiercer than the ravenous shark,
"A cry of hell-hounds' never-ceasing bark!"
And lo! the enormous giant to bedeck,
A golden millstone hangs upon his neck!
On him ambition's vulture darts her claws,
And with voracious rage his liver gnaws.
Our patriot comes! — the buckles of whose shoes
Not Cromwell's self was worthy to unloose.
Repeat his name in thunder to the skies!

14

Ye hills fall prostrate, and ye vales arise!
Through faction's wilderness prepare the way!
Prepare, ye listening senates, to obey!
The idol of the mob, behold him stand,
The alpha and omega of the land!
  Methinks I hear the bellowing demagogue
Dumb-sounding declamations disembogue,
Expressions of immeasurable length,
Where pompous jargon fills the place of strength;
Where fulminating, rumbling eloquence,
With loud theatric rage, bombards the sense;
And words, deep rank'd in horrible array,
Exasperated metaphors convey!
With these auxiliaries,, drawn up at large,
He bids enraged sedition beat the charge;
From England's sanguine hope his aid withdraws,
And lists to guide in insurrection's cause.
And lo! where, in her sacrilegious hand,
The parricide lifts high her burning brand!
Go, while she yet suspends her impious aim,
With those infernal lungs arouse the flame!
Though England merits not her least regard,
Thy friendly voice gold boxes shall reward!
Arise, embark! prepare thy martial car,
To lead her armies and provoke the war!

Rebellion wakes, impatient of delay,
The signal her black ensigns to display.*

. . . .

To thee, whose soul, all steadfast and serene,
Beholds the tumults that distract our scene
And, in the calmer seats of wisdom placed,
Enjoys the sweets of sentiment and taste;
To thee, O Marius! whom no factions sway,
The impartial muse devotes her honest lay!

---

* Luca Pitt continued at Florence, presuming upon his late alliance, and the promises which Pietro had made him; . . . . . But amongst all the changes that ensued upon this revolution, nothing was more remarkable than the case of Luca Pitt, who soon began to experience the difference betwixt prosperity and adversity, betwixt living in authority and falling into disgrace. His house, which used to be crowded with swarms of followers and dependants, was now as unfrequented as a desert; and his friends and relations were not only afraid of being seen with him, but durst not even salute him if they met him in the street; some of them having been deprived of their honours, others of their estates, and all of them threatened.

The magnificent palaces which he had begun to build were abandoned by the workmen; the services he had formerly done to any one were requited with injuries and abuse; and the honours he had conferred, with infamy and taunts. Many who had made him valuable presents, now came to demand them again, as only lent; and others, who before used to flatter and extol him to the skies, in these circumstances, loaded him with contumely, and reproaches of ingratitude, and violence; so that he heartily repented, though too late, that he had not followed Nicolo Soderini's advice, and preferred an honourable death to a life of ignominy and contempt.—Mach. Hist. Flor.

In her fond breast no prostituted aim,
Nor venal hope, assumes fair friendship's name:
Sooner shall Churchill's feeble meteor-ray,
That led our foundering demagogue astray,
Darkling to grope and flounce in error's night,
Eclipse great Mansfield's strong meridian light,
Than shall the change of fortune, time, or place,
Thy generous friendship in my heart efface!
O! whether wandering from thy country far,
And plunged amid the murdering scenes of war;
Or in the blest retreat of virtue laid,
Where contemplation spreads her awful shade;
If ever to forget thee I have power,
May Heaven desert me at my latest hour!
  Still satire bids my bosom beat to arms,
And throb with irresistible alarms.
Like some full river charged with falling showers,
Still o'er my breast her swelling deluge pours.
But rest and silence now, who wait beside,
With their strong flood-gates bar the impetuous tide.

. . . .

A POEM,

SACRED TO THE MEMORY OF HIS ROYAL HIGHNESS FREDERIC PRINCE OF WALES.

FROM the big horror of war's hoarse alarms,
And the tremendous clang of clashing arms,
Descend, my muse! a deeper scene to draw
(A scene will hold the listening world in awe)*
Is my intent: Melpomene inspire,
While, with sad notes, I strike the trembling lyre!
And may my lines with easy motion flow,
Melt as they move, and fill each heart with woe:
Big with the sorrow it describes, my song,
In solemn pomp, majestic, move along.
Oh! bear me to some awful silent glade
Where cedars form an unremitting shade;
Where never track of human feet was known;
Where never cheerful light of Phœbus shone;
Where chirping linnets warble tales of love,

* By awe, here, is meant attention.

And hoarser winds howl murmuring thro' the grove;
Where some unhappy wretch aye mourns his doom,
Deep melancholy wandering through the gloom;
Where solitude and meditation roam,
And where no dawning glimpse of hope can come;
Place me in such an unfrequented shade,
To speak to none but with the mighty dead:
To assist the pouring rains with brimful eyes,
And aid hoarse howling Boreas with my sighs.
When winter's horrors left Britannia's isle,
And spring in blooming verdure 'gan to smile;
When rills, unbound, began to purl along,
And warbling larks renew'd the vernal song;
When sprouting roses, deck'd in crimson dye,
Began to bloom, ...
Hard fate! then, noble Frederic, didst thou die:
Doom'd by inexorable fate's decree,
The approaching summer ne'er on earth to see;
In thy parch'd vitals burning fevers rage,
Whose flame the virtue of no herbs assuage;
No cooling medicine can its heat allay,
Relentless destiny cries, "No delay."
Ye powers! and must a prince so noble die?
(Whose equal breathes not under the ambient sky:)
Ah! must he die, then, in youth's full-blown prime,
Cut by the scythe of all-devouring time?

Yes, fate has doom'd! his soul now leaves its weight,
And all are under the decree of fate;
The irrevocable doom of destiny
Pronounced, "All mortals must submissive die."
The princes wait around with weeping eyes,
And the dome echoes all with piercing cries;
With doleful noise the matrons scream around,
With female shrieks the vaulted roofs rebound:
A dismal noise! Now one promiscuous roar
Cries, "Ah! the noble Frederic is no more!"
The chief reluctant yields his latest breath;
His eye-lids settle in the shades of death:
Dark sable shades present before each eye,
And the deep vast abyss, eternity!
Through perpetuity's expanse he springs;
And o'er the vast profound he shoots on wings:
The soul to distant regions steers her flight,
And sails incumbent on inferior night:
With vast celerity she shoots away,
And meets the regions of eternal day,
To shine for ever in the heavenly birth,
And leave the body here to rot on earth.
The melancholy patriots round it wait,
And mourn the royal hero's timeless fate.
Disconsolate they move, a mournful band!
In solemn pomp they march along the strand:

The noble chief, interr'd in youthful bloom,
Lies in the dreary regions of the tomb.
 Adown Augusta's pallid visage flow
The living pearls with unaffected woe:
Disconsolate, hapless, see pale Britain mourn,
Abandon'd isle! forsaken and forlorn!
With desperate hands her bleeding breast she beats;
While o'er her, frowning, grim destruction threats.
She mourns with heart-felt grief, she rends her hair,
And fills with piercing cries the echoing air.
Well may'st thou mourn thy patriot's timeless end,
Thy muse's patron, and thy merchant's friend.
What heart shall pity thy full-flowing grief?
What hand now deign to give thy poor relief?
To encourage arts, whose bounty now shall flow,
And learned science to promote, bestow?
Who now protect thee from the hostile frown,
And to the injured just return his own?
From usury and oppression who shall guard
The helpless, and the threatening ruin ward?
Alas! the truly noble Briton 's gone,
And left us here in ceaseless woe to moan!
Impending desolation hangs around,
And ruin hovers o'er the trembling ground:
The blooming spring droops her enamell'd head,
Her glories wither, and her flowers all fade:

The sprouting leaves already drop away;
Languish the living herbs with pale decay:
The bowing trees, see! o'er the blasted heath,
Depending, bend beneath the weight of death:
Wrapp'd in the expansive gloom, the lightnings play,
Hoarse thunder mutters through the aërial way:
All nature feels the pangs, the storms renew,
And sprouts, with fatal haste, the baleful yew.
Some power avert the threatening horrid weight,
And, godlike, prop Britannia's sinking state!
Minerva, hover o'er young George's soul;
May sacred wisdom all his deeds control!
Exalted grandeur in each action shine,
His conduct all declare the youth divine.
Methinks I see him shine a glorious star,
Gentle in peace, but terrible in war!
Methinks each region does his praise resound,
And nations tremble at his name around!
His fame, through every distant kingdom rung,
Proclaims him of the race from whence he sprung:
So sable smoke, in volumes curls on high,
Heaps roll on heaps, and blacken all the sky:
Already so, his fame, methinks, is hurl'd
Around the admiring venerating world.
So the benighted wanderer, on his way,
Laments the absence of all-cheering day;

Far distant from his friends and native home,
And not one glimpse does glimmer thro' the gloom:
In thought he breathes, each sigh his latest breath,
Present, each meditation, pits of death:
Irregular, wild chimeras fill his soul,
And death, and dying, every step control.
Till from the east there breaks a purple gleam,
His fears then vanish as a fleeting dream.
Hid in a cloud the sun first shoots his ray,
Then breaks effulgent on the illumined day;
We see no spot then in the flaming rays,
Confused and lost within the excessive blaze.

ODE ON THE DUKE OF YORK'S SECOND

DEPARTURE FROM ENGLAND
AS REAR ADMIRAL. WRITTEN ABOARD THE
ROYAL GEORGE.

Again the royal streamers play!
To glory Edward hastes away;
Adieu, ye happy silvan bowers,
Where pleasure's sprightly throng await!
Ye domes, where regal grandeur towers
In purple ornaments of state!
Ye scenes where virtue's sacred strain
Bids the tragic muse complain!
Where satire treads the comic stage,
To scourge and mend a venal age;
Where music pours the soft, melodious lay,
And melting symphonies congenial play!
Ye silken sons of ease, who dwell
In flowery vales of peace, farewell!
In vain the goddess of the myrtle grove
Her charms ineffable displays;
In vain she calls to happier realms of love,
Which Spring's unfading bloom arrays:

In vain her living roses blow,
And ever-vernal pleasures grow;
The gentle sports of youth no more
Allure him to the peaceful shore:
Arcadian ease no longer charms,
For war and fame alone can please.
His throbbing bosom beats to arms,
To war the hero moves, thro' storms and wintry seas.

CHORUS.

The gentle sports of youth no more
Allure him to the peaceful shore,
For war and fame alone can please;
To war the hero moves, thro' storms and wintry seas.

Though danger's hostile train appears
To thwart the course that honour steers;
Unmoved he leads the rugged way,
Despising peril and dismay:
His country calls; to guard her laws,
Lo! every joy the gallant youth resigns;
The avenging naval sword he draws,
And o'er the waves conducts her martial lines:
Hark! his sprightly clarions play;
Follow where he leads the way!

The piercing fife, the sounding drum,
Tell the deeps their master's come.

CHORUS.

Hark! his sprightly clarions play,
Follow where he leads the way!
The piercing fife, the sounding drum,
Tell the deeps their master's come.

Thus Alcmena's warlike son
The thorny course of virtue run,
When, taught by her unerring voice,
He made the glorious choice:
Severe, indeed, the attempt he knew,
Youth's genial ardours to subdue:
For pleasure, Venus' lovely form assumed;
Her glowing charms, divinely bright,
In all the pride of beauty bloom'd,
And struck his ravish'd sight.
Transfix'd, amazed,
Alcides gazed:
Enchanting grace
Adorn'd her face,
And all his changing looks confest
The alternate passions in his breast:
Her swelling bosom half reveal'd,

Her eyes that kindling raptures fir'd,
A thousand tender pains instill'd,
A thousand flatt'ring thoughts inspired:
Persuasion's sweetest language hung
In melting accent on her tongue:
Deep in his heart, the winning tale
Infused a magic power;
She prest him to the rosy vale,
And show'd the Elysian bower:
Her hand, that trembling ardours move,
Conducts him blushing to the blest alcove:
Ah! see, o'erpower'd by beauty's charms,
And won by love's resistless arms,
The captive yields to nature's soft alarms!

CHORUS.

Ah! see, o'erpower'd by beauty's charms,
And won by love's resistless arms,
The captive yields to nature's soft alarms!

Assist, ye guardian powers above!
From ruin save the son of Jove!
By heavenly mandate virtue came,
And check'd the fatal flame:
Swift as the quivering needle wheels,
Whose point the magnet's influence feels,

Inspired with awe,
He, turning, saw
The nymph divine
Transcendent shine;
And, while he view'd the godlike maid,
His heart a sacred impulse sway'd:
His eyes with ardent motion roll,
And love, regret, and hope, divide his soul.
But soon her words his pain destroy,
And all the numbers of his heart,
Return'd by her celestial art,
Now swell'd to strains of nobler joy.
Instructed thus by virtue's lore,
His happy steps the realms explore
Where guilt and error are no more:
The clouds that veil'd his intellectual ray,
Before his breath dispelling, melt away:
Broke loose from pleasure's glittering chain,
He scorn'd her soft inglorious reign:
Convinced, resolved, to virtue then he turn'd,
And in his breast paternal glory burn'd.

CHORUS.

Broke loose from pleasure's glittering chain,
He scorn'd her soft inglorious reign:

Convinced, resolved, to virtue then he turn'd,
And in his breast paternal glory burn'd.

So when on Britain's other hope she shone,
Like him the royal youth she won:
Thus taught, he bids his fleets advance
To curb the power of Spain and France:
Aloft his martial ensigns flow,
And hark! his brazen trumpets blow!
The watery profound,
Awaked by the sound,
All trembles around:
While Edward o'er the azure fields
Fraternal wonder wields:
High on the deck behold he stands,
And views around his floating bands
In awful order join:
They, while the warlike trumpet's strain,
Deep sounding swells along the main,
Extend the embattled line.
Then Britain triumphantly saw
His armament ride
Supreme on the tide,
And o'er the vast ocean give law.

CHORUS.

Then Britain triumphantly saw
His armament ride
Supreme on the tide,
And o'er the vast ocean give law.

Now with shouting peals of joy,
The ships their horrid tubes display,
Tier over tier in terrible array,
And wait the signal to destroy:
The sails all burn to engage:
Hark! hark! their shouts arise,
And shake the vaulted skies!
Exulting with bacchanal rage.
Then, Neptune, the hero revere,
Whose power is superior to thine!
And, when his proud squadrons appear,
The trident and chariot resign!

CHORUS.

Then, Neptune, the hero revere,
Whose power is superior to thine!
And, when his proud squadrons appear,
The trident and chariot resign!

Albion, wake thy grateful voice!
Let thy hills and vales rejoice:
O'er remotest hostile regions
Thy victorious flags are known;
Thy resistless martial legions
Dreadful move from zone to zone;
Thy flaming bolts unerring roll,
And all the trembling globe control:
Thy seamen, invincibly true,
No menace, no fraud, can subdue:
To thy great trust
Severely just,
All dissonant strife they disclaim:
To meet the foe,
Their bosoms glow;
Who only are rivals in fame.

CHORUS.

Thy seamen, invincibly true,
No menace, no fraud can subdue:
All dissonant strife they disclaim,
And only are rivals in fame.

For Edward tune your harps, ye Nine!
Triumphant strike each living string,

For him, in ecstasy divine,
  Your choral Io Pæans sing!
For him your festive concerts breathe!
For him your flowery garlands wreathe!
  Wake! O wake the joyful song!
    Ye fauns of the woods,
    Ye nymphs of the floods,
  The musical current prolong!
Ye sylvans, that dance on the plain,
  To swell the grand chorus accord!
Ye tritons, that sport on the main,
  Exulting, acknowledge your lord!
Till all the wild numbers combined,
  That floating proclaim
  Our admiral's name,
In symphony roll on the wind!

CHORUS.

Wake! O wake the joyful song!
Ye sylvans, that dance on the plain,
Ye tritons, that sport on the main,
The musical current prolong!

O! while consenting Britons praise,
  These votive measures deign to hear!

For thee my muse awakes her lays,
For thee the unequal viol plays,
The tribute of a soul sincere.
Nor thou, illustrious chief, refuse
The incense of a nautic muse!
For ah! to whom shall Neptune's sons complain,
But him whose arms unrivall'd rule the main?
Deep on my grateful breast
Thy favour is imprest:
No happy son of wealth or fame
To court a royal patron came!
A hapless youth, whose vital page
Was one sad lengthen'd tale of woe,
Where ruthless fate, impelling tides of rage,
Bade wave on wave in dire succession flow,
To glittering stars and titled names unknown,
Preferr'd his suit to thee alone.
The tale your sacred pity moved;
You felt, consented, and approved.
Then touch my strings, ye blest Pierian quire!
Exalt to rapture every happy line!
My bosom kindle with Promethean fire!
And swell each note with energy divine.
No more to plaintive sounds of woe
Let the vocal numbers flow!

Perhaps the chief to whom I sing
  May yet ordain auspicious days,
  To wake the lyre with nobler lays,
And tune to war the nervous string.
For who, untaught in Neptune's school,
Though all the powers of genius he possess,
Though disciplined by classic rule,
  With daring pencil can display
The fight that thunders on the watery way,
  And all its horrid incidents express?
To him, my muse, these warlike strains belong!
Source of thy hope, and patron of thy song.

CHORUS.

To him, my muse, these warlike strains belong!
Source of thy hope, and patron of thy song.

THE FOND LOVER.

A BALLAD.

A NYMPH of every charm possess'd,
  That native virtue gives,
Within my bosom all confess'd,
  In bright idea lives.
For her my trembling numbers play
  Along the pathless deep,
While sadly social with my lay
  The winds in concert weep.

If beauty's sacred influence charms
  The rage of adverse fate,
Say why the pleasing soft alarms
  Such cruel pangs create?
Since all her thoughts by sense refined,
  Unartful truth express,
Say wherefore sense and truth are join'd
  To give my soul distress?

If when her blooming lips I press,
  Which vernal fragrance fills,
Through all my veins the sweet excess
  In trembling motion thrills;

Say whence this secret anguish grows,
  Congenial with my joy?
And why the touch, where pleasure glows
  Should vital peace destroy?

If when my fair, in melting song,
  Awakes the vocal lay,
Not all your notes, ye Phocian throng,
  Such pleasing sounds convey;
Thus wrapt all o'er with fondest love,
  Why heaves this broken sigh?
For then my blood forgets to move,
  I gaze, adore, and die.

Accept, my charming maid, the strain
  Which you alone inspire;
To thee the dying strings complain
  That quiver on my lyre.
O! give this bleeding bosom ease,
  That knows no joy but thee;
Teach me thy happy art to please,
  Or deign to love like me.

ON THE UNCOMMON SCARCITY OF POETRY

IN THE GENTLEMAN'S MAGAZINE FOR DECEMBER LAST, 1755, BY I. W., A SAILOR.

THE springs of Helicon can winter bind,
And chill the fervour of a poet's mind?
What though the lowering skies and driving storm
The scenes of nature wide around deform,
The birds no longer sing, nor roses blow,
And all the landscape lies conceal'd in snow;
Yet rigid winter still is known to spare
The brighter beauties of the lovely fair:
Ye lovely fair, your sacred influence bring,
And with your smiles anticipate the spring.
Yet what avails the smiles of lovely maids,
Or vernal suns that glad the flowery glades;
The wood's green foliage, or the varying scene
Of fields and lawns, and gliding streams between,
What, to the wretch whom harder fates ordain,
Through the long year to plough the stormy main!
No murmuring streams, no sound of distant sheep,
Or song of birds invite his eyes to sleep:

By toil exhausted, when he sinks to rest,
Beneath his sun-burnt head no flowers are prest:
Down on his deck his fainting limbs are laid,
No spreading trees dispense their cooling shade,
No zephyrs round his aching temples play,
No fragrant breezes noxious heats allay.
The rude rough wind which stern Æolus sends,
Drives on in blasts, and while it cools, offends.
He wakes, but hears no music from the grove;
No varied landscape courts his eye to rove.
O'er the wide main he looks to distant skies,
Where nought but waves on rolling waves arise;
The boundless view fatigues his aching sight,
Nor yields his eye one object of delight.
No "female face divine" with cheering smiles,
The lingering hours of dangerous toil beguiles.
Yet distant beauty oft his genius fires,
And oft with love of sacred song inspires.
E'en I, the least of all the tuneful train,
On the rough ocean try this artless strain,
Rouse then, ye bards, who happier fortunes prove,
And tune the lyre to nature or to love.

DESCRIPTION OF A NINETY GUN SHIP,

FROM THE GENTLEMAN'S MAGAZINE, MAY, 1759.

AMIDST a wood of oaks with canvas leaves,
Which form'd a floating forest on the waves,
There stood a tower, whose vast stupendous size
Rear'd its huge mast, and seem'd to gore the skies,
From which a bloody pendant stretch'd afar
Its comet-tail, denouncing ample war;
Two younger giants* of inferior height
Display'd their sporting streamers to the sight:
The base below, another island rose,
To pour Britannia's thunder on her foes:
With bulk immense, like Ætna, she surveys
Above the rest, the lesser Cyclades:
Profuse of gold, in lustre like the sun,
Splendid with regal luxury she shone,
Lavish in wealth, luxuriant in her pride,
Behold the gilded mass exulting ride!
Her curious prow divides the silver waves,
In the salt ooze her radiant sides she laves,

---

* Fore and mizzen masts.

From stem to stern, her wondrous length survey,
Rising a beauteous Venus from the sea;
Her stem, with naval drapery engraved,
Show'd mimic warriors, who the tempest braved;
Whose visage fierce defied the lashing surge,
Of Gallic pride the emblematic scourge.
Tremendous figures, lo! her stern displays,
And hold a pharos* of distinguish'd blaze;
By night it shines a star of brightest form,
To point her way, and light her through the storm:
See dread engagements pictured to the life,
See admirals maintain the glorious strife:
Here breathing images in painted ire,
Seem for their country's freedom to expire;
Victorious fleets the flying fleets pursue,
Here strikes a ship, and there exults a crew:
A frigate here blows up with hideous glare,
And adds fresh terrors to the bleeding war.
But leaving feigned ornaments, behold!
Eight hundred youths of heart and sinew bold,
Mount up her shrouds, or to her tops ascend,
Some haul her braces, some her foresail bend;
Full ninety brazen guns her port-holes fill,
Ready with nitrous magazines to kill,

---

* Her poop lanthorn.

From dread embrasures formidably peep,
And seem to threaten ruin to the deep;
On pivots fix'd, the well-ranged swivels lie,
Or to point downward, or to brave the sky;
While peteraroes swell with infant rage,
Prepared, though small, with fury to engage.
Thus arm'd, may Britain long her state maintain,
And with triumphant navies rule the main.

THE END.

www.ingramcontent.com/pod-product-compliance
Lightning Source LLC
LaVergne TN
LVHW010233110826
845151LV00004B/1278
* 9 7 8 1 4 2 5 5 2 5 5 4 5 *